TWO LAWYERS
ONE DOCTOR

Breaking Barriers to Achieve Success

Cadine Bramwell

ISBN: 978-1-958443-57-6 (paperback)

Dedication

To our father, Charles Rory Bramwell, aka "Dada," who saw greatness within us long before we ever did. Your stars have fulfilled your wishes and are shining bright no matter what.

To our pillars of strength, our mother, Pauline, and our sister, Racquel, who always lift us up with unwavering love and support.

Foreword

This is a book about tenacity and resilience. It's about turning hopelessness into hope, converting the smallest opening into life-changing possibilities, and rejection into new opened doors. It's about changing the perception of having limited prospects to achieving limitless performance on the global stage. This is the lived experience of the book's author, Cadine Bramwell, as she and her triplet sisters pursued their future thoughtfully and purposefully, never taking no for an answer.

I first met Cadine Bramwell and her sisters when they applied to participate in the scholarship program sponsored by my Rotary Club of St. Andrew, based in Kingston, Jamaica, while I was President of the club in 2011/2012. Having grown up in Jamaica myself and having pursued my tertiary education in the United States, including receiving my MBA from the Harvard Business School, I had no doubt that the Bramwell triplets had what it took to reach their full potential starting with studying overseas. They each had an uncommonly high level of ambition coupled with an extraordinary capacity for hard work. I also saw in them a special willingness to think strategically about their options in life, as well as to pivot and refocus their energies with discipline when circumstances called for change. It was an honor for me to assist in facilitating the Bramwells accessing key resources for making it into and through the United States university system.

In **Two Lawyers One Doctor**, Ms. Bramwell does two things. Firstly, she takes the reader through a detailed and very interesting anecdote-filled account of how she and her sisters navigated their circumstances and opportunities to achieve their current academic and professional successes. This provides useful perspectives on how they overcame the many obstacles they faced almost at every turn throughout their journey.

Secondly, she presents a well-researched, step-by-step template for Caribbean students, especially those whose families have limited financial resources, for effectively enabling themselves to gain admission to United States colleges and universities and to access the required scholarships and other funding to facilitate their tertiary education success in the United States.

Robert A. Drummond
Kingston, Jamaica

Acknowledgements

Where would we be if it had not been for God on our side? On countless occasions, the Bramwell Triplets did not know how they would make it across the finish line, becoming two lawyers and a doctor. In these troubling moments, our faith in God funded the journey. Faith is simply believing that God has already worked it out, so we operate as though what we believe God for has already happened. This is faith to fund the journey, and it was a prerequisite for our success.

In tandem with our faith in the journey, my sisters and I are indelibly marked by the generosity and support we received from:

- Corporate Jamaica - Robert Drummond and the Rotary Club of St. Andrew, Jamaica; Sandra Bramwell and Versan Educational Services; GraceKennedy Limited; First Global Financial Services Limited; Paul Simpson and Cornerstone United Holdings Jamaica Limited.

- Church Community - Bishop Herro and Alma Blair and the Faith Cathedral Deliverance family; Pastor John Mark Bartlett and the Pentecostal Tabernacle family; Roderick and Dorothy Ferguson; Bishop Alton and Melony Samuels and the Full Gospel Tabernacle of Faith family.

Because of your investment in our education, we have defied the status quo, despite hailing from one of the most impoverished, violence-stricken communities in Jamaica.

The Calculated Chance

While delivering her final address as first lady of the United States, Michelle Obama said, *"When you are struggling and you start thinking about giving up, I want you to remember the power of hope. The belief that something better is always possible, if you are willing to work for it and fight for it. If we work hard enough and believe in ourselves, then we can be whatever we dream."*

When I reflect on my own journey, and the many obstacles that my sisters and I had to overcome to become two lawyers and one doctor, I wholeheartedly agree with former first lady Michelle Obama's power of hope message. However, when I consider my early teenage years, the constant hardships of life left me hopeless. Growing up in a poverty-stricken community and watching those around me always finding it hard to make ends meet, I struggled to believe that I was going to be any different. Since there were no lawyers or doctors around me that I could look up to as a tangible representation of what was possible for someone like me living in a run-down community, there was a season when I gave up before even trying. Truthfully, I did not know how to become something I had never seen. For this reason, representation matters.

When the Oscar-winning actress, Viola Davis, was asked why representation matters, she responded, *"Because you need to see a physical manifestation of your dream. There is something about seeing someone who looks like you that makes it [your dream] more tangible. You can see it; you can touch it. It gives you possibility."*

While living in the inner-city, I saw someone faced with similar hardships like me fight for their education and succeed, and it sparked hope within me. This lifeline of hope gave me possibility. I really needed to see that. Once I became hopeful, I began to believe in myself and started fighting for my education. Although I still lived in a low-income community and attended a low-income high school, I began believing that I could go from a low-performing student to a high-achieving student; thus, I began taking my academics seriously despite the hardships I faced. This is the power of hope; it changes you, even though your external situation does not change.

On the journey of pursuing your dreams, there will be many barriers. Sometimes, the barrier is affordability; other times, the barrier is accessibility. Perhaps, for you, achieving your dream is both unaffordable and inaccessible. If you are in this situation, does this mean your dream is unachievable? ABSOLUTELY NOT! Rather, you need to be flexible in your approach to achieve your dreams. As Bryant McGill rightly said, *"Rejection is merely redirection."* You can achieve your dream despite the barriers you may face, but it will likely be one hell of a fight (it sure was for my sisters and me).

Given that achieving your dreams is no easy task, what can you do to position yourself to come out on the winning side, regardless of the barriers you may face? You can take a calculated chance. A calculated chance is a term I coined to describe the Bramwell Triplet's ability to become successful professionals despite the many barriers in the way. A calculated chance occurs when you take intentional actions to increase the likelihood of you achieving your dream. In other words, the calculated chance is about intentionally positioning yourself in a manner that makes you become an opportunity magnet. Did you know that one intentional act can produce a domino effect that allows you to take advantage of life-changing opportunities? That's right, I said life-changing opportunities. Think rags to riches, literally. By no means is the calculated chance a game. Rather, the calculated chance requires you to be hopeful in hardships, strategically pivot when necessary, and never quit on your dreams.

In the preceding chapters, you will read of the Bramwell Triplet's calculated chance and the many barriers that had to be broken for my sisters and I to become two lawyers and one doctor. May it give you hope and possibility.

Table of Contents

Introduction

When the doctor told our mother that she was going to have twins, she did what any woman expecting twins would do: she bought two of everything she could afford. The normal gestation period elapsed; naturally, it was time to give birth. Our mother delivered two beautiful baby girls and was quite proud of all her efforts. As she attempted to relax, she heard the doctor exclaim, *"Another one!"* There was another baby in the womb! While our mother struggled to find the strength to deliver the third baby, our father collapsed on the hospital floor when he learned he was the father of not two but three identical girls, each weighing only three pounds. Once our father recovered from his initial shock, he proudly went on to name his triplet girls Cadine, Colleen, and Colliet Bramwell, and our parents made their way home with us.

Home for my sisters and me was a two-bedroom apartment in Tivoli Gardens, a notorious and marginalized inner-city community in Jamaica, West Indies. As young children, we spent our days in blissful ignorance of the stigmatization that plagued our community. Our father worked as a welder, and our mother was a housekeeper. Whatever money they earned was used to take care of us. While attending primary school, my sisters and I began understanding the severity of the financial woes gripping our low-income family. We were not as privileged as other kids. We did not have the luxury of purchasing school lunch consistently. Our parents could not give us lunch money on several occasions, so we walked home, ate, and returned to school.

One day, my sisters and I were at our primary school with no lunch money, and the torrential rain prevented us from walking home for lunch. Our mother was resolute that we would not go without food, so she sent our older brother with the pakchoi and white rice she made for our lunch. I also recall another day we went home for lunch, and when I saw our mother had prepared callaloo and white rice, I complained that I was tired of eating callaloo and longed for something delicious to eat. I pondered eating some curried chicken-back and white rice. It would have been a better alternative than the callaloo. However, even chicken back was simply too expensive for our low-income family at that time.

On the evening of that same day, I overheard my mother telling my father, *'Charlie, the pickney dem tiad a callaloo.'* As he heard the news, my father ashamedly bowed his head and sighed deeply. Witnessing my father's sigh of utter defeat, I knew that my complaint cut him deep. My father's sigh was the reprimand I needed to stop complaining about the food my parents worked tirelessly to provide. My father's pain humbled me, and I realized that I needed to be grateful that at least I had something to eat, regardless of whether it was callaloo, pakchoi or cabbage. I loved my father dearly, so I consciously decided to stop complaining about eating callaloo for breakfast, lunch, and dinner. Overclouded with remorse, I climbed the ladder that led to the rooftop of our four-story building and, staring into the night brilliantly lit by the numerous stars that stretched across the sky, I remembered my father's words to my sisters and me, *"Triplet, uno a star that shine bright nuh matta what!"*

As a young child, I did not feel like a bright star that shined no matter what. In fact, how could I when my environment was shrouded with crime, poverty, and hopelessness? Without shining star examples, how was I supposed to shine brightly? Was it by taking my academics seriously? If that were the case, then I would be in big trouble because

I found school boring and would rather play than study. Suffice it to say, for years, I did not understand what my father meant when he said I was a star that shined brightly no matter what.

Given that I was not academically ambitious (and neither were my sisters), I approached my primary studies haphazardly, and we ended up at a high school that was a short walk from our home. At high school, I stumbled upon examples of inner-city students shining brightly in their academics, and I suddenly began to have an appetite for academic success. This was the first time I was deeply inspired to take my academics seriously. Though I was inspired, I silently doubted whether I possessed the skills to succeed in high school because, for most of my life, I had lived among family and friends who never made it to high school or dropped out of high school because of teenage pregnancy, drugs, crime, lack of finances, or simply lack of interest. In other words, I was dealing with an intergenerational issue.

Battling with a limiting mindset, I took baby steps and crawled my way to becoming academically fit. Academic baby steps were simple things such as not missing classes and ensuring I completed whatever homework my teachers assigned. The remarkable beauty of crawling academically is that, despite my environment, I eventually developed an academically fit mindset strong enough to walk, jump, skip, and run after a better life for myself and my family. My sisters and I broke the generational curse of failing high school and collectively graduated with 31 Caribbean Secondary Examination Certificate (CSEC) subjects. Our CSEC success positioned us to take advantage of a life-changing opportunity to study in the United States on scholarships. Today, Colliet and I are lawyers, while Colleen is a medical doctor.

Structure of the Book

This book is divided into two parts and further subdivided into nine chapters. Part One of this book is written to show the calculated chance the Bramwell Triplets took to become two lawyers and one doctor despite the barriers in the way. Recognizing the incredible doors of opportunities studying in the United States provides, Part Two of this book is written for low-income Caribbean students in high school desiring to study in the United States. If you are a low-income student in high school, I hope the insightful strategies provided in Part Two (that is (i) positioning for academic success; (ii) participating in valuable extracurricular leadership activities; (iii) building a top-tier United States college/university application; (iv) tackling the SAT even if you cannot afford a private SAT prep course or a private SAT tutor; (v) using your SAT score as a compass and choosing the best United States college/university for you; (vi) obtaining employment while studying in the United States; and (vii) transitioning from international student to foreign professional in the United States) equips you with the primary tools needed to take advantage of the opportunities studying the United States provides.

Studying in the United States on scholarships is an incredible opportunity. However, I want to make it abundantly clear that this is only one of many amazing opportunities to obtain a tertiary education. If you are a student, it is your responsibility to be in a place where you become a scholarship opportunity magnet, maximizing and capitalizing on scholastic opportunities, whether they arise in your home country or abroad. To become a scholarship opportunity magnet and increase your likelihood of being a recipient of a tertiary scholarship (including local scholarships) that will help you obtain a tertiary education, you must spend your time in high school building a record that reflects your strong value of education and how you positively contributed to your high school community, despite a myriad of barriers that you may be faced with.

As I share my sisters' and my journey of becoming two lawyers and one doctor, I hope that our personal experiences of never giving up on the road to achieving our dream will empower Caribbean youths, especially low-income students in impoverished and marginalized inner-city communities, to see that they too can achieve great success.

Part I
The Bramwell Triplet's Calculated Chance

Chapter 1

The Tivoli Gardens Triplet

From early childhood to adulthood, the inner-city breaks most people it touches through the hardships they encounter. The greatest hardship is usually financial, which is the predecessor of the egregious acts of violence that plague inner-city communities. Financial hardship and inequitable access to resources cause inner-city parents to send their children to public (primary) schools instead of expensive private (preparatory) schools. As a result, children from the inner-city usually attend public schools within walking distance from their homes and often perform poorly on the national high school entrance exam (now called the Primary Exit Profile in Jamaica). They are then placed in high schools, referred to as non-traditional high schools with inadequate resources. This is the norm for many youths from the inner-city, and my sisters and I were not exempt.

As inner-city youths, my sisters and I attended Denham Town Primary School, which was only a short walk from home. There, the three of us performed poorly on the national high school entrance test (at the time, it was the Grade Six Achievement Test (GSAT)) and were placed at Tivoli Gardens High School, which is considered a non-traditional high school in Jamaica. Unsurprisingly, several of our friends who performed poorly on the GSAT were also placed at the school or another similar non-traditional high school. When I consider the reason for our low performance on GSAT, I think we simply did not value our education as young children. Frankly, we loved playing with our friends and watching television much more than our classwork. My father was highly disappointed with us for not attending traditional high schools. Ironically, attending a non-traditional high school, like Tivoli Gardens High School, was a blessing in disguise. Tivoli Gardens High School's motto is to bloom where you are planted. Though we graduated from primary school as low-performing students, if we took our studies there seriously, we could bloom into high-achieving students.

Colliet and I were in class 7A, while Colleen was in class 7B. We were not athletically inclined, so we did not participate in any athletic activities outside the required physical education classes. However, we were socially inclined, so we all joined our high school's Peer Educator Club. At the time, our guidance counsellor was the club's facilitator, and Colliet was voted the student president. Our high school guidance counsellor played an influential role in the redevelopment of our academic ambitions. Through the Peer Educator Club, our guidance counsellor exposed us to positive life practices that eventually shaped our leadership and communication skills. As peer educators, we attended several educational programs outside the regular school hours. We were also responsible for sponsoring various programs that allowed us to share the knowledge we gained with our peers. As our leadership responsibilities at school increased, our appetite for good grades grew. We gradually developed a routine of staying late at school for peer educators' meetings and for completing various class assignments.

For the first time in the history of our secondary education, we did well on our grade 7 internal end-of-year examinations, and we were all placed in class 8A. This meant we outperformed our peers that did not get placed in class 8A. Because we were in the same classroom, there were many occasions when our teachers were unable to tell the three of us apart, which was quite understandable given that members of our own family occasionally got us confused. Our teachers decided that we had to wear name tags to help them differentiate us. We reluctantly agreed to wear the name tags, although none of the other students in our class had to wear them. To be fair, there were no other triplets in our class. To help our teachers differentiate us further, we never sat together during class time. During our entire grade 8 tenure, Colliet sat on the left side of the classroom, Colleen sat on the right side, and I sat in the middle of the classroom.

As we became well-rounded high schoolers, we continued to do well on our internal examinations and eventually transitioned to class 9A, where we no longer needed to wear any name tags, thankfully. When we started grade 9, we were notified that a friend's sister passed eight CSEC subjects in her final year at the school. Her success was the talk of the new school term. This was the first time I had ever heard of a student from a non-traditional high school like Tivoli Gardens succeeding in eight CSECs in grade 11. In my astonishment, I secretly wondered if perhaps she just got lucky. Or maybe she was simply brilliant.

Shortly after, I learned that another student at the school also passed eight CSECs in grade 11. I was flabbergasted at the news. How in heaven did these girls do it? Whatever those two students had done to obtain such stellar CSEC results, I craved it. Truthfully, the idea of succeeding in eight CSEC subjects in grade 11 felt preposterous. Though I was doing well in my academics, as I transitioned from one grade to the next, I was not yet at a place where I was confident in my ability to excel in one CSEC subject, much less 8 CSEC subjects. As I mentioned before, the inner-city breaks most people that it touches, and I was a broken inner-city girl intimidated by the thought of success. CSEC exams were uncharted territories for me, and I simply doubted my ability to excel in them. Though doubts permeated my mind, these two inner-city students' CSEC success stories planted seeds of hope in my garden of doubts.

At the start of the grade 9 academic year, I learned that a social studies teacher offered after-school lessons to students preparing for the social studies CSEC exams. Initially, I did not think much of this because I had two more years until I had to worry about CSEC exams. However, as the story of the two inner-city students who had done exceptionally well on their CSEC exams resonated in my heart, I pondered how to produce similar CSEC results. As stated earlier, taking 8 CSEC subjects in grade 11 was very intimidating. I wondered what would happen if I took the CSEC exams incrementally. Given that I was a complete novice in taking (and passing) CSEC subjects, I knew I needed to select only one CSEC subject that was manageable. Social Studies felt like a good subject to get my foot in the door, so I (along with my sisters) paid the necessary fees and registered for the social studies CSEC exam. This meant we were at least committed when the time came. However, we were so occupied with studying for our grade 9 internal examinations and our extra-curricular activities that we did not devote much time to studying for the social studies CSEC exam.

We finished the first term of grade 9 very strong—we came second, third, and fourth in our class. Our future was becoming increasingly academically ambitious, and our parents were extremely proud of us. In March 2009, the Jamaica Observer wrote an article about us titled, *"Triple the Fun - Inner-City Trio Impresses Teachers, Do Well in School."* The article highlighted how we were each blooming at Tivoli Gardens High School. On the day that the Jamaica Observer issued our story, our father told us that he had just boarded a JUTC bus when he saw our picture in the newspaper that the bus conductor was reading. As the proud father that he was, he could not keep the excitement to himself, and so he was very quick to point out to the bus conductor that those triplet girls in the newspaper were his daughters—his 'stars' to be exact.

As the social studies CSEC exam approached, we tried to study for this exam and prepare for our regular classwork. We constantly feared that we had not acquired enough knowledge to pass this exam. Regardless of our fear of failure, we had already paid for the exam, and there was no escaping it. The days leading up to our social studies CSEC exam were simply terrifying. A few of my classmates also studying for this exam would sometimes stay late at school with us to study. One particular afternoon, when we stayed late at school, one of our teachers decided to test our social studies knowledge by giving us a pop quiz. Given that we were only days away from the exam, we were grateful that the teacher was willing to take the time to ask us questions. Less than thirty minutes into the pop quiz, I regretted it. I did not know the answer to most of the questions! I came out of that session feeling worse than when I entered. With only a few days remaining until it was time to take the social studies CSEC exam, the pop quiz confirmed my fears; I was not ready. Seeing I could not escape this exam, my only option was to use the few days I had to 'cram' as much information on this topic as I could, which exactly what I did.

On the day of the social studies CSEC exam, we got to school very early without having breakfast. As the adrenaline was rampant throughout our bodies, it was easy to forget we were taking this important exam on an empty stomach. As we waited for the social studies examiner to distribute the paper, anxiety permeated a room already tensed and stifling. It was as though I had taken on a major academic burden, and everything I had experienced up until this moment was not enough to prepare me for the desired success. By the time I finished the exam, an overwhelming sense of relief satiated my mind. Regardless of whether I had done enough to pass the exam, I was simply grateful to be finished. When the social studies CSEC results were released, an immediate feeling of sickness filled the pit of my stomach. The hour of truth came, and although I was eager to get my results, it was also terrifying to think that I did not pass. Eventually, we summoned the courage to walk to school to retrieve our results. By the time we got to school, we had noticed a line of students waiting to be called by the guidance counsellor for their CSEC results. When the guidance counsellor eventually called us for our results, we walked over to her shakily, and she informed us that all three of us had passed the social studies CSEC exam. Colliet got a grade I on the exam, while Colleen and I got a grade II on the exam. My sisters and I were extremely happy that none of us had failed the exam. It was an inner-city trio success!

By the time we started grade 10, we each had a CSEC subject under our belts. This was something that many of our peers were unable to say. This was the motivation for us to go after another CSEC subject. This time, we chose human and social biology. In addition to human and social biology, I decided to take the physical education CSEC exam. Similar to our busy schedule in grade 9, we continued with our peer educators' activities and continued doing well on our internal examinations. One of the immediate challenges I realized with human and social biology was my difficulty in comprehending the biology area. This meant I needed to dedicate more time and effort to obtain similar CSEC results as before.

At the end of the first term of grade 10, we were preparing for our internal examination when we got the heart-wrenching news that our father was murdered. We were fifteen, and it felt as though our hearts had been yanked from our bodies. Despite such devastating news, our internal exams were days away from commencing, so we had to study, even if that meant with tears in our eyes. Days leading up to our internal exams, some of our high school teachers visited our small two-bedroom home in Tivoli, where they found us in different corners of our home studying for the upcoming end-of-year exams. To them, in that moment, we had displayed an acute determination that failure was not an option for us, even amid grief and pain. This reflected the daughters our father had raised us to be; his stars that would shine no matter what. Excelling in our academics was our way of honoring our father, so we studied. Sometimes, we paused our studies and sobbed because the pain that our father was never coming home again was debilitating. However, we never stopped studying until our mother told us that our teachers had decided to excuse us from the grade 10 end-of-term exams. Apparently, our teachers were so moved when they witnessed us attempting to study in our grief-stricken state that they all agreed it was too much for us, so we got the time to grieve our beloved father.

At the start of 2010, we returned to school with a deep conviction to continue excelling in our academics. With the loss of our father, our mother now had the overwhelming responsibility of figuring out how she would provide for us. It was difficult for our family, especially since our mother's main occupation was housekeeping, which only paid a meager salary. For as long as I can remember, our parents always had an issue finding lunch money for us to attend school. With our mother as the sole breadwinner of the family, this challenge was exacerbated. During this difficult time, our church community rallied together to provide our mother with monthly stipends to help cover our school expenses. Our guidance counsellor also encouraged our mother to apply for the Path Program, which was funded by the Jamaican government, to assist us with obtaining free lunches up to three times a week. This may seem like an insignificant gesture to some, but for us, it was extremely comforting knowing that we did not have to worry about finding lunch for at least three of the five days we were at school.

Amidst the personal challenges plaguing my family, I was happy to resume the final term of grade 10. Aside from maintaining good grades, I was keen on carving out time to study for the upcoming CSEC exams. At the beginning of studying for the human and social biology exam, we had a determination to learn the necessary materials on our own. However, it became very clear to us that we also needed additional help to understand the different concepts in the textbook. Unfortunately, we did not have the money to pay for any after-school private lessons. We needed a good, knowledgeable Samaritan with the time to teach us human and social biology for free. For a while, this good Samaritan was nowhere to be found, so we had to continue doing our best on our own.

As it was customary for us to stay late at school, we gradually became familiar with the different groups of people who also stayed at school late. During one of those after-school evenings, I was talking casually with another inner-city student who was in his final year, and I vented to him my frustration with human and social biology. During this conversation, he told me he would be willing to teach us everything he knew about the subject on Saturdays. He thought this was a good way to also improve his ability to perform well on the exam. It was essentially a quid pro quo situation; we needed someone to teach us for free, and he was mastering the subject by teaching us. It was agreed that we would meet our student-teacher every Saturday for three hours, and he would review everything he had learned with us for that week.

When the first Saturday came, all three of us, along with two of our friends from the inner-city, arrived on time, ready for our free lessons. It was truly remarkable and inspiring witnessing one of my own peers, who was also from the inner-city, take his academics so seriously, to the point that he did not just want to do enough to pass;

he desired a grade I in each of his upcoming CSEC exams—a very ambitious aspiration.

We made sure to prioritize our weekend activities so that we never had to miss any Saturday lessons. We were grateful for this opportunity because having someone expound on some of the more complex areas in human and social biology made comprehending the subject much more palatable. Ironically, our student-teacher soon shared his frustration with us because he was of the view that we were not retaining the information he so diligently taught us. It appeared to him that we were reading just to say we reviewed the material. We did not take the initiative to go the extra mile, summarize key concepts, or complete all the textbook quizzes at the end of each chapter, which our student-teacher challenged us to do. According to our student-teacher, retaining the information in each chapter of the textbook was extremely important. Although this made sense to us, it meant that we needed to carve out more time to focus on retaining the information we had been passively reading.

To retain the information in the human and social biology textbook, we would retire to bed early and wake up in the middle of the night to study. This was no easy task. There were many nights I would wake up with the intent to study and, by the time, I opened my textbooks, I fell asleep. Gradually, I learned that the most I could study for was an hour to an hour and a half. I also found that sitting on the cold concrete floor was best because the discomfort helped me stay awake. Eventually, we had a consistent routine of waking up in the night and sitting on the concrete floor of our respective corners in the kitchen and the living room area, reading through the chapters, summarizing key concepts, completing the pop quizzes at the end of the chapters, and then reviewing the answers. We were so consistent with this routine that even our student-teacher could tell that we were doing better, which made teaching more beneficial because he did not have to repeat himself as much.

I was confident I would perform well on the human and social biology exam. After all, I finished the textbook chapters, including all the quizzes, and always attended the Saturday sessions. I was proud of the ambitious student I became in preparation for this exam. To my dismay, when I completed the human and social biology exam, I left the exam room as though I was leaving a funeral procession. The exam was hard, and I needed to mourn because I was not confident I performed well enough to pass. I crawled my way home and bawled my eyes out because I was convinced I failed the exam, despite all the hard work and preparation. When the CSEC results were released, we were not in a rush to get them. In some ways, we wanted to delay any news of failure. Eventually, we had to collect our results if, for no other reason, our mother would not rest until we told her how we did on the exam. To our utter relief and our mother's sheer happiness, all three of us passed human and social biology with a grade I. I also passed the Physical Education CSEC exam with a grade II. Those nights of studying on the cold concrete floor were all worth it. This meant that we were collectively going into our final year of high school with seven CSEC subjects. I completed grade 10 knowing that I survived one of the darkest periods of my life, and like my father always told us, we shined like stars no matter our circumstances. Though this was an extremely challenging year, I craved academic success, so I developed grit and pursued my academic ambitions.

It was a bittersweet moment when we got to grade 11. Sweet because we were in our final year of high school, but bitter because we had more CSEC subjects to take and no specific post-high school plans. At the start of the grade 11 academic year, our mother shared with our guidance school counsellor that she did not know how she would pay for us to attend college simultaneously. The desire to attend college was borne by each of us, but this was not an easy task, especially when our mother barely had enough money for us to buy lunch at school. How would she ever pay college tuition for not one but all three of us—it seemed virtually impossible! As our mother shared her plight with our guidance counsellor, she gracefully reassured her that we simply needed to continue doing well academically and that by doing so, we could potentially obtain scholarships to help with our college tuition. Though it felt like wishful thinking, it planted a seed of hope and comforted our mother that perhaps the three of us could attend college simultaneously.

Although we had already secured seven CSEC subjects collectively, we needed to take additional subjects in grade 11. Since I was familiar with the CSEC exams, I was mindful of the discipline required to succeed in each. The incremental steps of taking one CSEC subject each academic year showed me that I could achieve academic success. Given that I had secured three CSEC subjects, I had the option to take five subjects, which would result in me securing eight CSEC subjects by the time I graduated high school. Although I had the option to do fewer, I desired to sit eight CSEC subjects in grade 11. My academic ambitions had changed; I was no longer a low-performing student. I had grown into a high-achieving inner-city student because I was confident in my ability to perform well in my CSEC exams. Ironically, my sisters also decided to sit eight CSEC subjects in grade 11.

We were in our final year of high school, so our mother would regularly discuss our plans post-high school with us. Truthfully, I felt more prepared for my CSEC exams and had not given much thought to plans after high school. I knew I had a deep desire to further my studies, but my thoughts were often preoccupied with the exorbitant costs and my mother's inability to cover it. After considering the overwhelming cost of college, Colleen and Colliet decided to apply to teacher's college because it was cheaper than attending the University of West Indies, Mona, or the University of Technology, Jamaica. I, on the other hand, needed a clear plan on what to study. I knew I wanted a good-paying job; anything that would pay me enough to take our mother out of Tivoli Gardens.

While we continued to prepare for our CSEC exams, our mother encouraged me to apply for the engineering program at the University of Technology, Jamaica in hopes that I could make good money as an engineer. I should have explained to my mother that mathematics was my most challenging subject, so my future as an engineer did not look promising. While Colleen and Colliet successfully applied for teachers' college, I did not pass the University of Technology entrance exam for its engineering program. Truthfully, this was somewhat expected. During the entrance exam, which consisted mainly of mathematical questions, I recall attempting to solve some of the questions and not seeing my answers among the answer choices on the exam paper. This was a clear sign. I was not going to pass the exam. With the engineering program no longer a viable option, I had no idea what I would do next.

During my final months of high school, I had no clear plans post-high school. Coincidentally, the Rotary Club of St. Andrew, Jamaica sent a letter to Tivoli Gardens High School notifying our principal that they were looking for five high-performing students to apply for an opportunity to study in the United States. A few days later, our principal brought us into her office and told us about the Rotary Club's scholarship opportunity. I remember when our guidance counsellor told our mother not to worry about how we would afford college. She reassured our mother that if we continued to do well on our exams, we could possibly get scholarships to attend college. It was as though our guidance counsellor was a visionary. Just as she predicted, a major scholarship opportunity was presented to us: a scholarship opportunity to study in the United States!

Our excitement about the scholarship opportunity ended when our principal told us that only one of us could apply for the scholarship. Apparently, only five students could be selected from the entire school population. Although we were well qualified, it would not be considered fair for her to choose all three of us because we came from the same household. This was understandable, so we agreed that I should apply for the scholarship since I did not have any plans post-high school. If I successfully applied for the scholarship, it would mean that our mother would only have to worry about Colleen and Colliet's college tuition. The thought of lessening our mother's financial burden motivated me to commit to doing whatever I needed to get the scholarship. As our father would say, the Bramwell Triplets are stars that shine no matter what, and I was ready to shine.

Chapter II

Succeeding in High School

High School will be whatever you make of it. Some students only attend high school because a parent or guardian forces them to go. School is a social gathering for these students, and they will spend most of their time idling with friends. There are some students who attend high school because it is a family requirement, and there is an innate academic interest—a great driving force that pushes them to give keen attention to their studies. Lastly, some students attend high school with the potential to excel academically. Still, these students spend most of their time only doing the bare minimum to remain in good academic standing at school. These students have much untapped academic potential, and they make up many of the classrooms of the high schools in the different inner-city communities across Jamaica and the Caribbean.

My sisters and I had to overcome a myriad of socio-economic challenges to succeed in high school as low-income students from a notorious inner-city community. Inner-city communities, like ours, are filled with high school dropouts who failed to tap into their full capabilities. Many high school dropouts fall prey to gun violence and gang participation, teenage pregnancy, and drug use. I knew many high school dropouts who were victims of the cycle of poverty and deprivation that permeated communities like Tivoli Gardens. I strongly believe that these men and women could have turned out differently had they continued their studies. Many high-school dropouts also spend their lives earning minimum wages that can barely take care of themselves and their families. I knew many families who were financially unstable because they did not possess the educational skills and qualifications to secure high-paying jobs. Sadly, this is the lived experience of many in the inner-city communities across Jamaica and the Caribbean.

We were not strangers to gun violence. It was our lived experience. However, we learned early on from our parents how to adjust and not be affected by it. Several incidents of gun violence caused us to shift our placement in our small two-bedroom home whenever necessary, and we avoided the windows so we could study amid the gunshots. From primary school to high school, there were several occasions where shoot-outs and drive-by shootings interrupted our school activities, and we were dismissed from school early. On some occasions, despite the early dismissal, we remained at school because the walk from school could be deadly, as it was not safe due to the ongoing unrest. This was the life we were accustomed to as inner-city youths.

In May 2010, residents of the Tivoli Gardens community experienced one of the most horrific and deadly incursions between West Kingston gunmen and the Jamaican Defense Force. A few days before the incursion, our mother told us that she was sending us to our older sister, who lived in Portmore—a suburb outside of Kingston. Our safety was her priority, and our home, she feared, was no longer safe for us. Although we escaped the horrors of the incursions, our mother, brother, aunts, uncle, cousins, friends, and classmates had to suffer through the invasion. Men were brutally dragged from their homes by the Jamaican Defense Force, and some were allowed to return home after extensive interrogations. However, several of these men never returned home. They were shot and killed. During the bloody invasion, our cousin's mother was shot and killed, and her body was left to rot on the street for days.

We returned home after the incursion when it was safe. We returned to a community where many of the buildings now had gunshot holes. Death and uneasiness lingered in the air as though the incursion was not over. Grief and trauma seemed like it would never depart from the residents of the West Kingston community. Some of our classmates experienced the incursion, and resuming high school was no easy task for these students. For some, returning to high school was an arduous battle as they struggled with the incursion's lingering effects, which impacted their mental health. The silver lining for some students, including my sisters and me, was an undeniable yearning to graduate high school as high-achieving students. The adage that education is the ticket out of poverty finally resonated with many of us. After enduring gun violence and financial hardship, we were motivated to use education to dig ourselves out of the misery of the inner-city.

In almost every inner-city community, there is a minority group of outliers who will defeat the odds and fight to make something good of themselves. This minority group shatters the curse of generational poverty. These outliers are survivors. They endure the trauma and stigmatization and use education as a catalyst to become lawyers, doctors, nurses, teachers, accountants, etc. A crucial commonality between the majority and the minority is that both groups have access to the same 24 hours a day. The distinguishing trait between these two groups of people is time management. Admittedly, when we were in primary school, we were not academically ambitious and squandered our time in school. Fortunately, we experienced a series of events at high school, and our academic posture drastically improved. As high schoolers, we learned that our greatest asset was time management, so we became good stewards of our time in school.

In my final year of high school, I was selected to compete for the Rotary Club of St. Andrew scholarship program. I was tasked with writing an essay explaining why I believed I should be chosen. The essay's questions were daunting because there were other low-income high school students whose lives had also been tainted by poverty, hardship, and violence. I feared that I did not have much uniqueness to write about. Deciding how to differentiate myself was not readily apparent. I wrote an essay about being the firstborn of a triplet in Tivoli Gardens, attending Tivoli Gardens High School, and dealing with the aftermath of my father's death and the Tivoli Gardens incursion. I explained that I was not always a hardworking student, and at the beginning of high school, the idea that I could take eight CSEC exams in my final year of high school and pass all of them was, in my opinion, unthinkable. However, my high school's Peer Educator Club helped to reshape my academic aspirations. As a low-income student, I was aware that my education was my shovel, and I would use it to dig myself and my family out of the inner-city. I had already secured three CSEC subjects when I started grade 11, and I was confident that I would score high in all eight of the remaining CSEC subjects that I was scheduled to sit in my final year of high school.

The Rotary Club of St. Andrew found my essay persuasive and transitioned me to the second round of the scholarship competition—the interviews round. The Rotary Club of St. Andrew held interviews at the Pegasus Hotel in Kingston. The four other students and I from Tivoli Gardens High School travelled together for the interview. Upon my arrival at the Pegasus Hotel, it was clear that other students had travelled far and near to vie for the scholarship. All the students appeared well qualified—well, they must have been to have made it this far in the competition. The students, who were well dressed in their uniforms, appeared to be the crème de la crème from their respective high schools. The "imposter syndrome" kicked in, and it was enough to unsettle me. My hands were sweating profusely, and my heart was beating so rapidly that if someone came close to me, they could hear it. Despite the various nerve-racking reactions in my body, I strode into the interview room with a big, bright smile. After introducing myself, I sat down expecting that the interviewer, Sandra Bramwell (no relation to us), a counsellor for overseas study and the Executive Director of Versan Educational Services, would interrogate me intensely. To my surprise, the interview felt more like a conversation. As the interviewer asked questions about my family and high school tenure, I shared my experiences and motivation for deciding to take CSEC subjects from grade 9. Although not intentional, I mentioned my sisters in so many of my responses that the interviewer began asking about Colleen and Colliet, as though I was being interviewed on behalf of the Bramwell Triplets. By the end of the conversation, I was quite confident that I would be selected for the second round of interviews.

At the end of the first round of interviews, I rejoined the large group of high school students waiting to find out if they were moving on to the second round of interviews. As soon as I returned to the large group, so did my nervousness, sweatiness, and feebleness. This group of students intimidated me because they were a constant reminder of how competitive the process was. I wondered if I had accomplished enough to persuade the interviewers that I deserved the scholarship. As soon as the interviewer joined the large group of high school students, all conversations among the students ceased. The only thing that mattered at that moment was finding out who was selected for the next round of interviews. With all eyes glazed on the interviewer, the students listened intently as the interviewer began calling out the names of the students who were moving forward. Eventually, my name was called, as well as two other students from Tivoli Gardens High School, and we were all taken to a conference room where the second round of interviews would be conducted. As the interviewer for the second round of interviews, Robert Drummond, the then President of the Rotary Club of St. Andrew, stepped into the conference room, my nervousness started compounding by the second. The defining moment had finally arrived, and those who made it to the second round could sense it. As pangs of uneasiness engulfed me, I became worried and pondered on what else was left to share to persuade the interviewer that I was the perfect candidate for the scholarship.

My interview with Mr. Drummond was brief and straightforward. The interviewer focused primarily on whether I could manage college in the United States, especially without my sisters, with whom I shared a strong bond. Admittedly, I had never been separated from my sisters, and so attending school in a new country, away from my sisters, was unchartered territory. I was mindful to explain that being away from my family was a price I was willing and ready to pay to obtain my college degree. When the interview was over, I remained in the conference room until the other two Tivoli Gardens High School candidates completed their interviews. Although I could not hear the conversation of the remaining candidates who were being interviewed from my seat, the other students were doing an exceptional job of persuading the interviewer that they were ideal candidates for the scholarship. Both the interviewer and the students appeared to be having a good conversation. I thought about how lacking this was in my interview. It caused me to doubt whether my interview was successful. After a tiring day, I left the Pegasus Hotel uncertain if I had outperformed my peers.

By the time all interviews were completed, torrential rain drenched me on my way home. With feelings of exhaustion and uncertainty, I desperately wanted to make it home to enjoy some of my mother's cooking and spend the rest of the day relaxing with my sisters. As I walked through the door, my heart sank at the sight of buckets all over our small two-bedroom apartment, collecting raindrops from the leaking ceiling. After many years of living in the same apartment, we knew that torrential rain meant we would be uncomfortable for several days until the water ran off our roof. Although this was our routine during the hurricane seasons, as I watched the rain droplets seep from the holes in our ceiling, tears of frustration began to escape from my eyes. In truth, my tears were an outward expression of tiredness, both with the ceiling that seemed like it would never get fixed and, more importantly, stark fear that I had not done enough to convince the interviewers to select me for the scholarship, which also meant I had not done enough to dig my way out of the muck and mire of the inner-city.

Not long after the interview, one of my classmates called me, screaming that the President of the Rotary Club of St. Andrew informed her she had been selected to participate in the scholarship. This was amazing news for my classmate, another inner-city youth well acquainted with the hardships that plagued low-income students. Excitedly, she then asked me if the President had called me, to which I responded *"Not yet."* Immediately, there was an awkward silence; no one wanted to say anything to give false hope, and eventually, the call ended with a promise that I would let her know if the President called me. Luckily, I did not have to spend much time lamenting over the lack of a call because, within that same hour, the President of the Rotary Club of St. Andrew called me to congratulate me for being selected to participate in the scholarship. When I got the good news, I bowed my head as uncontrollable tears of joy flowed from my eyes. Soon, I was not the only one crying. My mother joined in with me because she understood that all our lives had changed, and it had changed for the good. At that moment, my mother and I sat on the cold concrete floor and cried together. The child who had no post-high school plans and the struggling single mother who did not know how she was going to afford college tuition for her triplet girls had a reason to celebrate: her firstborn of the triplets was going to attend college in the United States.

When the news that two of the five candidates from Tivoli Gardens High School were selected to participate in the Rotary Club of St. Andrew scholarship opportunity was shared amongst the original group of students who vied for the scholarship, they were all happy that at least two students were successful. However, my classmates who were not selected for the scholarship had an unshakable urge to see if anything could be done to salvage what appeared to be a lost battle. One of my classmates googled the address for Versan Educational Services and suggested we visit Ms. Bramwell to find out if there were any other scholarship opportunities. Although I had already been selected for the Rotary scholarship, I went along with the group as moral support. I also convinced my sisters to tag along on the journey, so eight of us from Tivoli Gardens High School travelled to Versan. We scraped together the few coins we had to ensure there was enough money to cover everyone's roundtrip bus fare.

My classmates had no plans or persuasive words to convince Ms. Bramwell to assist them with securing any other available scholarships, especially since she had already interviewed all of them except for Colleen and Colliet. They were just students from the inner-city who were hungry for an education and had nothing to lose except for their pride; they wanted to see if there was anything that she could do to help them. The possibility of Ms. Bramwell being able to help my classmates who were not successful with the Rotary scholarship was enough motivation to make us overlook the fact that the sun was vehemently beating on us, and amongst the eight of us, there was not enough money to stop and buy bottled water for all of us.

Although my classmates and I did not have an appointment with Ms. Bramwell, we bravely entered Versan's office, intent on waiting however long it took to meet with Ms. Bramwell. Granted, Ms. Bramwell was quite surprised to see the eight of us in her office fumbling with our words as we asked for help. Ms. Bramwell spoke to my classmates with much generosity and sympathy. Although Ms. Bramwell was unable to provide any further assistance to my classmates who were not successful with the Rotary scholarship, she told Colleen and Colliet that Mr. Drummond was conducting additional interviews at the Pegasus Hotel, and they should see if they could get an impromptu interview with him. Although there was no guarantee they would be able to speak with Mr. Drummond, they gladly jumped at the possibility of him speaking to them, even if they had to wait until he finished speaking with all the other high school candidates who were scheduled for the day.

With no direct invitation to meet with Mr. Drummond, Colleen and Colliet hurried over to Pegasus Hotel, eager to seek out an opportunity to speak with Mr. Drummond. My classmate, who was also successful with the Rotary scholarship, tagged along. When we got to the Pegasus Hotel, my classmate and I quickly realized that we could not explain our reason for being at the hotel since we had already done our interviews, so we remained by the roadside while Colleen and Colliet found a way to speak with Mr. Drummond. Colleen and Colliet were the only students not wearing school uniforms, and it caused them to stand out. It made them uncomfortable because they looked as though they were not prepared for such an important occasion. Regardless of their shortcomings, Colliet and Colleen waited patiently until Mr. Drummond completed all his scheduled interviews with the high schoolers. Before Mr. Drummond could leave the conference room, Colleen and Colliet brisked up their pace and met with him. When Colleen and Colliet explained they were my sisters, a conversation struck up, and Mr.

Drummond was delighted to meet the other two Bramwell sisters. Aside from the almost identical physical features, Mr. Drummond realized my sister's academic success in high school was identical to mine. After the meeting with Mr. Drummond, they left Pegasus Hotel with bright smiles and rejoined my classmate and me, sitting on the road pavement as the scorching sun beat against our skin. My sisters' interview resulted in positive feedback, and now they simply had to wait to see the outcome.

When I received my official letter from the Rotary Club of St. Andrew congratulating me for being selected as a candidate for the scholarship program, the first sentence of the letter stated, *"Success is where opportunity meets preparation."* Grateful to have been chosen for the scholarship program, the statement resonated with me deeply. Weeks passed between the time I received my initial call informing me I had been selected, to when I received my official scholarship letter. Within those weeks, CSEC results had been released, and thankfully, my sisters and I received mainly grade I and grade II on our exams, except for mathematics. Colliet and I failed the subject, but luckily, this did not jeopardize my scholarship because I retook the exam and passed before starting college in the United States. Unfortunately, I had colleagues who were initially part of the scholarship, but their CSEC results were not on par with the opportunity, and they could no longer continue the program. As one can imagine, this was heart-wrenching for these students—a missed opportunity to transform their lives. We, however, learned a lot from the experience.

I vividly recall my conversation with my friend, who was removed from the scholarship opportunity minutes after she learned she could no longer continue with the program. It was a bleak Saturday afternoon, and we had just completed SAT classes sponsored by Versan Educational Service. After classes, we boarded a coaster bus to downtown where we would trek to West Kingston. As we sat together on the bus, my teary friend told me that she wished she had taken her studies more seriously. A once-in-a-lifetime opportunity had presented itself, and she was not prepared. If she had known that this scholarship opportunity would present itself in grade 11, she would have taken her academics much more seriously. She missed her golden opportunity to go to college for free. This was painful. There were no words to encourage her because the harsh reality was, she could not go back in time and change things. It was a rare phenomenon. Usually, low-income students in Jamaica and the Caribbean struggle to attend college mainly because they lack financial resources to pay their college tuition. Sitting beside me was someone with the opportunity, but she lacked the CSEC performance scores and had to forgo her ticket to study in the United States.

While my friend dealt with sharp pangs of remorse over her CSEC grades, my sisters' CSEC grades, which were mainly grade I and grade II, catapulted them into the Rotary scholarship program. The Rotary Club of St. Andrew extended official letters to Colleen and Colliet to join the scholarship program, and they gladly accepted the offers. Their tenacity and a deep desire for betterment brought them to a place where we could all now study in the United States together. I learned from this experience how critical it is for high school students, particularly low-income high schoolers, to position themselves to excel in their CSEC exams. Success truly takes place when preparation meets opportunity, and low-income students in Jamaica and the Caribbean need to prepare for academic success.

Chapter III

Triple the Success

Our scholarship program through the Rotary Club of St. Andrew included SAT prep courses provided by Versan Educational Services. As young girls who lived in an inner-city community our entire lives and had only attended schools there, classes at Versan Educational Services felt like a breath of fresh air. Most of the students looked like they were from affluent families, and most attended traditional high schools. Our poverty-stricken background made it easy for us to feel like strangers in a foreign land. Despite our high achievements with CSEC exams, the SAT proved to be an uphill battle for us. Now that we had graduated high school and were unemployed, we opted for the summer months following our high school graduation to study for the SAT. We had approximately three months to focus solely on excelling on the SAT exam, which was an extremely challenging test for us.

The SAT can be considered a gatekeeper that differentiates those who will attend top-ranking colleges and universities in the United States with scholarships. At the time, we needed to score at least 1800 on the SAT to vie for a full college or university scholarship in the United States. Our mock SAT results often showed that we were nowhere close to the 1800 benchmark we needed, and it made us feel as though our dreams to study in the United States were shattered. Occasionally, our scores would increase by a few points. However, it was still not enough. It was as though my academic growth plateaued. During that period, when I felt my academic growth was at a standstill, I had a friend at church who had recently completed Versan Educational Services a few months earlier and was preparing to leave Jamaica to attend Columbia University on a full scholarship. Columbia is a prestigious university in New York. Her SAT score was well above the 1800 benchmark, and I was simply in awe of her stellar accomplishment. She epitomized the college dream that appeared to be slipping away from me.

As our fate seemed doomed by our mediocre SAT scores, we did not know how to fix our bleak situation. When we sat the actual SAT exam, our scores were very similar to our mediocre mock exams, and we were utterly devastated. Given that we did not score within the range that we needed, we instantly assumed that it meant that college in the United States was no longer a viable option. The reality that we were now back to square one was debilitating, and our hopes for a brighter future beyond our inner-city community were now obliviated. Failure was a difficult pill for us to swallow because it meant that we were not coming out of the inner-city. A well-known quote by W. Clement Stone says, *"Aim for the moon. If you miss it, you may hit a star."* Our moon was getting at least 1800 on the SAT, and we failed to do so. However, we were pleasantly surprised when Robert Drummond, the President of the Rotary Club of St. Andrew, informed us that our hopes of attending college in the United States were not lost despite our SAT scores. His words of hope trickled into the depths of my bleeding heart and pulled me out of despair. I did not have all the details at the time, but the fact that he said there were some options for us was sufficient to keep my faith alive.

With guidance from the founder of Versan Educational Services, Sandra Bramwell, and Robert Drummond, we were very strategic with the United States colleges and universities we applied for. Strategic, in this sense, meant applying to accredited colleges and universities where we still had a good chance of receiving scholarships, even if the scholarships were not going to be full as we had initially hoped. This also meant that we wanted to be in a location where the tuition would not be overly expensive. This was particularly important because a partial scholarship meant that we would be responsible for out-of-pocket expenses. Since there were three of us, those expenses would be triple the burden for our single-parent family. Although we understood that our chances of receiving a full scholarship to a United States college were unlikely since our SAT scores were not as competitive as they needed to be, we were grateful that those who were guiding us throughout the journey still believed that we could at least receive partial scholarships to attend college in the United States.

At the time, we had limited knowledge about the various colleges and universities across the 50 states in the United States. I did not have an ideal college or university I wanted to attend; I just knew I wanted to attend college in the United States on a scholarship. As we gleaned guidance from Robert Drummond and Versan Educational Services, we learned about the difference between colleges located in southern states compared to northern states and the difference between Predominantly White Institutions (PWI) and Historically Black Colleges and Universities (HBCUs). Given that we had spent all our lives in one inner-city community, I realized that Robert Drummond was keen on ensuring that the college or university we attended would provide us with a culturally diversifying experience.

Eventually, we applied to approximately five colleges and universities in North Carolina. Though some United States colleges and universities require prospective students to do an interview as part of the college admission process, the colleges and universities to which we applied required no such interviews. As part of our United States college applications, we had to provide (and if you are a student aspiring to study in the United States, you will likely be required to provide the same) high school transcripts, letters of recommendation, SAT scores, and personal statements. As we prepared our personal statements for submission, the value of our extracurricular leadership activities (i.e., peer educators club) became evident.

Our personal statements gave us the opportunity to share things that were not readily apparent by merely looking at our transcripts or even our SAT scores. We could pull stories from the many times we had to fight for our education despite the various obstacles we faced at home and within our inner-city community. We also shared how we balanced our academics while participating in the Peer Educators Club. We learned that well-rounded students need a healthy mixture of educational and social forums to develop rapport and build camaraderie with their peers. Thankfully, we had several experiences that we could draw from.

One of the many programs we hosted through the Peer Educators Club was a canned food drive to help a senior home in our community, and we described the impact the project had on us. As peer educators, we also hosted a talent show and encouraged students to participate and compete for various prizes. We fundraised and supported the prizes with money from the tickets we sold to the talent show. Aside from our academic accomplishments, these extracurricular experiences helped us differentiate ourselves from other candidates.

Once we submitted our United States college applications, it felt like a weight was lifted off our shoulders, and we could relax, even momentarily. As weeks turned into months and I did not hear any response from any of the colleges I applied to, I became uneasy and, frankly, very worried. Given that I lived on the last floor of a four-story building, I could look through the kitchen window and see the mailman riding his bicycle along the stretch leading to our building. Whenever we saw the mailman at our building, one of us would hurriedly sprint down the flight of stairs in our building to collect the mail. We were greatly disappointed each time we realized that the mails were not from any of the United States colleges we had applied to. The mailman grew accustomed to our anticipation and sometimes would save us the trouble of sprinting down the stairs if he knew that he had no mail for us. On one occasion, our mother spotted the mailman a block from our house, and she checked with him to see if he had any good news for us, but sadly he did not. When she got home, she told us that she already checked with the mailman, and he did not have any mail for us. The waiting felt eternal.

One afternoon, I spotted the mailman riding along on his usual stretch, but this time, he was making a sound with his bicycle, almost as though he could not wait to get to our building because he had something for us. As soon as he got to our building, he shouted out, *"Triplet, mi have mail fi unnu,"* and at that moment, we knew it was from one of the colleges in the United States. With the brightest smiles, it was a race among the three of us to see who would get to him first.

Initially, we were so overjoyed that we did not realize that he only handed us two letters instead of three. When we returned to our house, and our beating hearts slowed, we opened the two letters addressed to Colliet and me from Saint Augustine's University in Raleigh, North Carolina congratulating us on our acceptance into the university. There was no such letter for Colleen, so the moment was bittersweet. It was very perplexing that Saint Augustine's University did not send any letter to Colleen. Given that there was no rejection letter, we attempted to reassure ourselves that Colleen's acceptance letter was surely on the way. Eventually, Colleen's letter from Saint Augustine's

University, and all the other colleges, came in the mail. We rejoiced because we all got accepted to a college in the United States!

In addition to receiving acceptance letters from Saint Augustine's University, we also received acceptance letters from most of the remaining colleges we applied to in North Carolina. In what felt like a blink of an eye, we were suddenly comparing the colleges against each other to determine which offer we should accept. Our admission letters from the different colleges made us feel unstoppable until the reality that none of the schools offered us full scholarships kicked in.

Although we had gone through so much from our CSEC days, SAT days, and college application days, we were now at a Red Sea that seemed uncrossable. How would we pay the remaining balance of any of the colleges we received acceptance offers from? The question was very daunting for us because it was abundantly clear that our single-parent family household did not have the financial bandwidth to carry this burden. It was very unsettling. We created a routine wherein we held meetings every morning to brainstorm how we could potentially secure additional scholarship funds and discuss all things college-related. We checked in with each other daily to see if there were any new emails or letters from any of the colleges regarding increasing our scholarship. These daily conversations kept us going through the many wretched weeks when we did not see where the funding to cover the deficit would come from.

During all the uncertainty that we faced as to how we would finance the remaining college tuition, Robert Drummond was increasingly becoming someone who was the epitome of a true mentor. He was aware of our financial plight, yet he seemingly never missed a beat to encourage us not to give up. Every encounter that we had with Mr. Drummond was an implicit reminder that things would eventually work out for us. Granted, this is real life, and the funds we need would not just fall from the sky and land in our hands. Instead, we needed to persuade those with financial capabilities to help us. If you think about it, we had to persuade the Rotary Club of St. Andrew to select us for their scholarship program (which they did), and we had to persuade the various colleges that we deserved a seat at their institution (with which most of them agreed), now we needed to do some persuasion to secure additional funds.

To secure additional scholarship funds, we emailed the colleges that accepted us, informing them that we were looking forward to attending their respective colleges; however, we needed additional scholarship funds to ensure we were a part of the upcoming first-year students. We sometimes followed up with phone calls in addition to sending emails to the colleges (whenever we could find the money to purchase calling credit). This task is not for the faint of heart because it is very easy to get discouraged when no one replies to your emails or returns your phone call, or worse, you get a response from a college that they are unable to provide any additional funds, aside from what has been initially awarded.

In one of the many status emails that we sent to the colleges to remind them how much we were looking forward to attending college in the fall and to see if there was any additional funding available, we finally got an email from the Johnson C. Smith University informing us that they were going to increase our scholarships amounts. Although it was still not a full scholarship, we were beyond happy. At this point, Johnson C. Smith offered us the most amount in scholarships, thus, we were very much inclined to accept their offer. Despite our recent success in increasing the amount of funding they awarded us, we still needed to secure more funding to close the gap.

Our mentor, Robert Drummond, was also the President of First Global Financial Services (FGFS), and he informed us of the arrangements he was making to meet with some folks at FGFS and its parent company, Grace Kennedy Limited (GK), to ask them to consider committing to covering the financial deficit left by Johnson C. Smith financial package. When Mr. Drummond shared this news with us, we were deeply moved because he was willing to go where we could not go and speak on our behalf. These were people in Jamaica with the financial capabilities to help make our dreams a reality. This was the most shocking encounter we had experienced on this journey. We always looked to sources (i.e., the colleges) in the United States as the only means to help us close the financial deficit. Given that we were not attending college locally, we never considered that we could secure additional funding from the land of our birth, our Jamaica.

I began punching the numbers in the calculator to determine how much Jamaican dollars we would need GK/FGFS to provide us with for the next four years. The amount of money we needed was a significant commitment, so I constantly questioned whether such an ask was out of reach. I remember feeling quite bleak when I realized the amount that each of us would require for the next four years. Thankfully, we were not going before the GK/FGFS team because, frankly, the amount of money we were asking for intimidated us.

The day Mr. Drummond met with the GK/FGFS team was one of the best days of my life. Though we were at home, we were mummified until we heard from him. Finally, he called and told us that GK/FGFS agreed to sponsor us. It was only by the grace of God that none of us fainted when we heard the good news! At that moment, we were so proud to be Jamaicans. Despite the significant amount we needed to cover our remaining college tuitions, a major Jamaican conglomerate agreed to sponsor us, and we were deeply humbled and indelibly grateful to them. This was a defining moment because we could finally have peace of mind knowing that our entire college tuition was now covered. The news of GK/FGFS's commitment gave us the keys out of the inner-city, and it was a moment that we would treasure for the rest of our lives.

When we thought that things could not get any better, it did. When we informed Saint Augustine's University that Johnson C. Smith University had increased our scholarship amount, they were willing to consider matching that amount. It was quite miraculous to know that two colleges in the United States were now vying for the Bramwell Triplets from Tivoli Gardens to attend their school. To our surprise, Saint Augustine's University decided to top Johnson C. Smith's scholarship offer, so we decided to go with them as they offered the most scholarships.

Chapter IV

Achieving the College Dream

Although my sisters and I received partial scholarships from Saint Augustine's University in Raleigh, North Carolina, which covered half our tuition, and GK/FGFS covered our remaining tuition fees, including room and board, there were a handful of miscellaneous expenses that we had to account for as international students. Before we arrived at Saint Augustine's University, the FGFS team met with our mother to discuss some final matters regarding our studies in the United States. The FGFS team explained to our mom that we would likely need pocket money to cover whatever expenses came up while studying, such as money for food, clothes, and social activities. Though there was no specific amount as to how much we would need for pocket money, it was our mother's responsibility to try to source this money.

Once our mother shared the news with us, we quickly reassured her that there was no need to worry about sending us any pocket money. The last thing we wanted was for our mother to start worrying about us. We were at a juncture in our lives where we had spent eighteen years in one of Jamaica's most notorious and poverty-stricken communities, so we knew how to push past whatever obstacles and get the work done. We were going to study in the United States on scholarships, and that was the only thing that mattered to us. With or without pocket money, we would be happy. At that moment, we were hungry for an education that broke generational curses, so pocket money for social activities was the least of our concerns.

Prior to leaving Jamaica, with very limited funds, our mother took us shopping downtown West Kingston, where she bargained the price with each vendor by explaining that we were triplets. My mother had a special knack for bargaining, and after explaining that she needed three of each item, the vendors cooperated and sold her the items at a discounted price. Sometimes, there are not enough words to describe an indescribable moment, and I have experienced quite a few. One of those moments happened when I sat in church and watched our pastor ask for a special offering to help my sisters and me purchase a laptop for studying in the United States. The church community was so receptive. It felt as though the entire congregation donated all they had to assist us. My eyes were a fountain of tears as I witnessed such an immeasurable gesture of kindness. We used the money to purchase a brand-new laptop for university, which we all shared.

Our flight on Delta Airlines to Raleigh, North Carolina, was an unforgettable experience, not because anything exciting happened; instead, it was the simple fact that after a long and arduous journey, we were finally crossing our Red Sea and going over to Canaan land. Our mentor, Robert Drummond, and his daughter who was starting her second year at a university in the United States, accompanied us, which was so very kind of them. Their presence made the experience less intimidating. Since it was the weekend and school did not officially start until Monday, our mentor arranged hotel accommodation for all of us. As I followed his guidance, I was in awe of my new environment. The air smelt fresh, the streets were clean, and I quickly became a fan of a fast-food restaurant called Chic-fil-A.

The very next day, Mr. Drummond drove us to Saint Augustine's University, and we toured the school and sat through various first-year activities, one of them being a pep rally. One of the amazing things that he did for us while visiting Saint Augustine's University was introducing us to the then-president and vice-presidents of the university. Though it was a very brief introduction, the university leaders were now aware that a set of triplets from Jamaica were attending the school on scholarships.

Mr. Drummond and his daughter took us shopping to get some essential supplies for school before we moved into our on-campus dorm room. We shopped at stores like Target and Walmart, and Mr. Drummond's rental car was full of all the purchases for our dorm rooms.

Prior to our campus arrival, we requested that the three of us share the same dorm room and were fortunate to have a room together with the addition of another student. The dorm rooms were set up so that two students could share a room with an adjoining bathroom shared with another dorm room. Colleen and I shared a dorm room, and Colliet's dorm room, which she shared with another student, was always easy to access because we could just walk through the bathroom, and there she was. Growing up in a small two-bedroom apartment in Tivoli Gardens, we had to share the same bed all our lives, so we each welcomed the ability to sleep in our own beds when we got to college. The downside of having our own beds for the first time meant we had to buy sheet sets and comforters for each bed, which tripled the bedding expenses.

In addition to bedding supplies, we needed a variety of clothes to wear throughout the four seasons of the year. From a financial perspective, purchasing clothes for the different seasons was intimidating, overwhelming, and expensive. This made me nostalgic about the good high school days in Jamaica, where we could wear the same uniforms all year long regardless of whether the uniform was old or new, even if we repeated the same uniforms from a previous grade. Though our mother was miles away in Jamaica, she relentlessly scraped together as much money as she could to help us purchase the items we needed for college. What she could not do herself, she never hesitated to ask for others to step in and assist. Our mother unashamedly reached out to our church community for our bedding supplies to see if anyone could assist us. On the eve of our first day of classes, one of our Sunday school teachers in Jamaica informed us that she ordered bedding supplies from Walmart and that they would be delivered before the week was out. We were tremendously blessed by this gesture.

In addition to the brand-new laptop and bedding supplies we received because of the financial assistance from our church community, our mentor, Robert Drummond, decided to purchase cell phones for us. In addition to purchasing the cell phones for the three of us, he graciously paid our monthly phone bills as we pursued our studies at Saint Augustine's University. On the eve of the start of the new semester, we had the opportunity to have dinner with Mr. Drummond's relatives, who were also Jamaicans living in the Raleigh area. The realization that they lived near our school and we could reach out to them if we ever needed to was extremely comforting. Eventually, dinner ended, and so did Mr. Drummond and his daughter's weekend trip to help get us settled in our new environment. When they dropped us off at Saint Augustine's University and bid us farewell, we were eager to begin our collegiate journey. We were planted at Saint Augustine's, and whether rain or shine, we would blossom.

We indeed blossomed! We thrived at Saint Augustine's University. Colleen majored in Biology, Colliet majored in Political Science with a minor in pre-law, and I majored in History with a minor in pre-law. Our university classes were relatively small, allowing us the opportunity to connect better with our peers and professors. Because we were accustomed to participating in student government activities at Tivoli Gardens High School, it was natural for us to seek student government opportunities within the first few weeks of starting university. Colliet competed for Student President of our freshman class and was successful. Similarly, Colleen competed for Freshman Class Queen and was successful. As a result, Colleen sat on the Queen's Council which required her to attend major school events. Additionally, Colleen had to participate in many community outreach programs. I served as Colliet's Chief of Staff throughout her tenure as student president. Having known her all her life, who could better champion and support her?

We were well-known in our freshman (first-year college students) year because of our government positions in our collegiate community. I realized that being actively engaged on campus not only helped us to be well-rounded students, but it also helped us to network with different people, especially living in a foreign land for the first time. Despite our various student government positions, we completed our first semester in college with strong grade point averages (i.e., a number that indicates how high you scored in a course on average, typically from 1.00 to 4.00). Colliet and I completed our semester with a 4.0 grade point average (GPA), while Colleen completed her first semester with a 3.7 GPA. We were excited about this for several reasons. First, our scholarships from Saint Augustine's University required us to maintain a certain GPA, and we were all well above the requirement. Second, despite our involvement in various extracurricular activities, we reported strong academic success to the individuals who invested in us. Lastly, our strong GPAs showed us that where we came from had no bearing on our ability to excel, even above our peers.

Within the first few weeks of university, I learned that a few job openings were posted throughout the campus. My initial reaction was sheer joy and relief because we still struggled to find money for miscellaneous expenses. My happiness about the on-campus job openings was brief because when I inquired about the positions, I learned that only United States citizens or permanent residents could apply. This was heartbreaking because of our financial constraints. The United States government paid the stipend that students would receive in exchange for working approximately 20 hours per week. Because of this, we did not qualify as we were international students. I remember sharing this news with my mother, and she was adamant that we had to find someone from the institution and plead our cause. Our mother's strong prompt reminded us of the relentless approach we took when we sought scholarships from Saint Augustine. We emailed the admissions departments about scholarships so often that they knew us by name, even if they were annoyed with us. The memory of how we persevered and went against the grain empowered us to not stop at what we heard. We had faith that a door could be opened amid the regulations.

The first person we attempted to speak with was the university's president. We believed we needed someone with authority to grant our request to work on campus as international students. Although we were not eligible for work-study since it was a government program, we could work on campus if the university was willing to pay us. Our attempt to meet with the president was unsuccessful as she had a very busy schedule. However, there was no way we would tell our mother we were unsuccessful, so we tried to get an audience with the next best person with authority, the vice president. As fate would have it, he remembered us from our introductory meeting with Mr. Drummond and happily agreed to meet. Though I cannot recall the decisive factor that convinced the vice president to grant our part-time work request, the Bramwell Triplets from Jamaica had made an impressionable impact, and he was willing to inquire about the next steps for us to work on campus. Mr. Drummond's intentional act of having us meet with our university leaders had paid off.

Our mother was relieved when we told her that the university finally agreed to let us work part-time on campus. This was unprecedented since we were the first international students ever to receive on-campus employment at our university. There were a handful of international students at our university, but many received either a full academic or a full athletic scholarship, which did not allow them to accept any on-campus employment. Given that we had only received partial scholarships from the university, we were allowed to work on campus when employment was available. Colleen and I worked in the vice president's office, while Colliet worked in the Student Business Department. Managing a part-time job, student government activities, and academic coursework was not easy. We had to be diligent stewards of our time to maintain strong grades while juggling our other commitments. We were very fortunate to be where we were, so we did what we had to, knowing that our hard work would not be in vain.

As we transitioned from one semester to the next, we continued participating in various extracurricular activities. Though we came from humble beginnings, we cultivated a reputation that distinguished us both inside and outside the classroom. We got accepted into our university's honors program, allowing us to take several advanced courses and participate in different community service projects. At one point, I served as President of the Honors Society. I had the opportunity to give remarks during honors convocation (i.e., an undergraduate ceremony recognizing students for distinguished academic achievements).

We were all settled on our career paths by the time we were sophomores (i.e., second-year college students). While Colliet and I decided to become lawyers while in college, Colleen had wanted to be a doctor from high school days. Once we knew our respective career paths, we began seeking internships that aligned with our goals. Some college students can obtain paid internships during the semester that align with their career goals. However, as international students, it was very challenging for us to obtain paid internships. In fact, many paid internships we came across often indicated that only United States citizens or permanent residents were eligible. As a result, the process proved difficult to obtain paid internships. Challenges were the norm for us at this point. Thankfully, we knew how to persevere and continuously search for opportunities that aligned with our interests.

Though we could not secure paid internships throughout the various semesters, ample non-paid internships aligned with our interests as pre-law and pre-med students. Thus, we were able to volunteer at a handful of organizations and gain much-needed experience and insight into our respective careers. Colliet and I volunteered at Common Cause, League of Conservatism, and the Equal Employment Opportunity Commission, while Colleen interned at the Duke Raleigh Hospital. Our volunteerism turned out to be well aligned with our resume-building objectives.

Throughout our sophomore year in university, we continued our search for paid summer internships. Eventually, we secured paid summer internships that aligned with our career goals and were not limited to only United States citizens or permanent residents. Colleen secured a clinical research summer internship program at Marshfield Clinic in Marshfield, Wisconsin, while Colliet and I participated in the Ronald H. Brown Pre-Law Program in Queens, New York, which allowed us to participate in law school classes and intern with state court judicial at New York City Criminal Court, Bronx Supreme Court, and Queens District Attorney's office. After an extremely rewarding summer in New York and Wisconsin, we returned to Saint Augustine's University to continue our academics.

For the remaining two years of university, we continued juggling our part-time on-campus jobs while managing increasingly demanding coursework and student government activities. We participated in different research programs, wrote papers on our findings, and presented at undergraduate research day (i.e., a day where undergraduate students showcase research, scholarship, and scholastic endeavors). We received several educational awards for academic excellence from our respective departments throughout our tenure at Saint Augustine's.

In 2016, Colliet and I graduated with Summa Cum Laude (i.e., we earned grades within the highest percentage of our departments), and Colleen graduated with Magna Cum Laude (i.e., she earned high grades within her department). As valedictorian of our graduating class, Colliet delivered a well-received farewell speech at our graduation. Our mother, older sister, and mentor, Robert Drummond, along with his cousin who lived in Raleigh, attended our graduation and witnessed us marching triumphantly to collect our bachelor's degrees that we worked so hard to achieve. Our college dream was graduating from Saint Augustine's with high honors and zero debt. After four years of devotion to our studies and collegiate community, our dream became our reality.

Chapter V

Life Beyond College

Graduating with our bachelor's degree from Saint Augustine University was a transformative experience. After graduation, we had the option to return to our home country and pursue work opportunities that aligned with your interests. We also had the option to further our studies at graduate school (e.g., pursuing a master's degree). Early in our collegiate journey, my sisters and I wanted to continue our studies. While Colliet and I desired to attend law school, Colleen wanted to attend medical school. By the first semester of the third year at university, we began exploring the various requirements for admission into our respective graduate programs. In addition to working hard to ensure we met the graduate program requirements, we had to figure out how to pay for these programs. Our best shot at affording graduate school was through scholarships. Unfortunately, the availability of scholarships for graduate school is generally very limited and competitive.

To gain admission into law and medical school, Colliet and I had to take the Law School Admission Test (LSAT), while Colleen had to take the Medical College Admission Test (MCAT). In many ways, the LSAT and MCAT were very similar to our SAT experience. Our scores on these exams were not competitive enough to receive full scholarships to our respective graduate programs. Though disappointing, giving up on graduate school was not an option. Colliet and I secured partial scholarships to the University of Florida Levin School of Law in Gainesville, Florida. A partial scholarship is always better than no scholarship, so we were thankful for the scholarships.

On the other hand, Colleen was admitted into Ross University School of Medicine (RUSM), a medical school in the Caribbean. Truthfully, our family had great concerns about Colleen's decision to leave the United States and attend RUSM in the island of Dominica. This was partly because Dominica was foreign to our family; we had no friends or relatives living there, and, more importantly, Colleen had not received any scholarships to cover her medical school expenses. These were all seemingly valid reasons for our loved ones to be concerned. Colleen, however, had an indomitable spirit. She finally got admitted to medical school, and there was no way she would not attend. She did not have the money but had faith to fund her medical school journey. Colleen's faith enabled her to board a flight to Dominica to start her first semester of medical school.

During orientation week at RSUM, an officer from the school's financial department asked Colleen how she would pay for medical school, and she replied, *'I am believing God to provide.'* The officer responded by saying, *'Okay, but when do you think God will provide?'* She did not know the answer to that question but hoped it would be soon. Despite the great uncertainties that Colleen faced, she attended her white coat ceremony (which is a ceremony for medical students where a white coat is placed on each student's shoulder signifying their entrance into the medical profession), and Colliet and I watched online. My eyes were a fountain of water as I watched Colleen's professor place her white coat on her. I was incredibly proud of my sister for facing her challenges head-on. Colleen may have been penniless at the time, but no one could tell as she looked so radiant in her white coat.

For an entire semester, Colleen visited her school's financial aid department to inquire about receiving assistance. She was met with constant rejection. The denial was disheartening, and there were many tears of frustration. Still, she would show up and ask the same question she asked the day before, hoping she would get good news one day. Some may have seen her as a nuisance, but she kept showing up. On days when repeated disappointments made her cry, faith made her rise from despair. On the brink of being evicted from medical school because of failure to make payment, Colleen miraculously received an email from her school's financial aid department that a loan was available to cover her tuition throughout her entire tenure at medical school. When she went to the financial aid department to apply for the loan, the officer told her they had her in mind when the loan was suddenly available because she always showed up regardless of the persistent rejections. By showing up every day, she made sure they did not forget her, and when the opportunity presented itself, they remembered her. As I like to say, God remembered her.

Somewhat different from Colleen's journey, Colliet and I remained in the United States after graduating college because we planned to attend UF Levin School of Law in Gainesville, Florida. Since the scholarships we received from the law school were only partial scholarships, Colliet and I were responsible for covering all remaining law school expenses. Before graduating from Saint Augustine's University, our designated school official (DSO) brought Colliet and I into her office to inquire about our post-college plans. At the time, I had no knowledge of optional practical training (OPT) and was focused only on going to law school. When Colliet and I explained to the DSO that we had already gotten accepted into law school, she recommended that we inquire with the law school about deferring for a year, and if the school agrees to it, we could use the year to work and save as much money as possible to help with our school fees. Before this conversation, Colliet and I had never considered OPT or the possibility of deferring law school for a year. Truthfully, we did not know that these options were available to us. We discussed a one-year deferral with UF Levin School of Law, particularly to confirm that our scholarships would not be affected, and they agreed. Although neither Colliet nor I had any job offers lined up, the idea of working for a year and saving as much money as possible to help with our expenses was exciting. Before graduating from Saint Augustine's University, Colliet secured employment near the university's campus. She remained in North Carolina for a year, working on OPT. I, on the other hand, struggled to secure employment before graduation. Thankfully, OPT does not require a job offer before receiving a work authorization card.

During my final year of university, I served as the President of the Student Honors Club, so I was required to speak at the school's annual honors convocation. At this event, a serendipitous exchange took place that changed my trajectory to law school. The keynote speaker was an alumna of Saint Augustine University and an attorney in New York. The university held a private luncheon following the convocation ceremony, and I recall only having a brief introduction with the keynote speaker. Unbeknownst to me at the time, that brief introduction left a strong impression on the attorney. After a few weeks, I received an email from the office of alumnae with a job offer from the attorney in New York. It was unbelievable how a seemingly small act (i.e., me speaking at an honors convocation) could produce such an amazing and unexpected opportunity. A job I had not even applied for was suddenly available, so immediately after graduation, I boarded the Greyhound bus to New York.

In New York, I was met with unexpected disappointments. My employment authorization card (EAD) got lost in the mail, and I could not work until I got a new card, which took almost a month to receive. Additionally, the legal assistant position I was initially offered was no longer available because the attorney had to fill the position. By the time I got my new EAD, I had to begin job hunting. It took almost four months for me to secure employment as an entry-level mailroom clerk at a personal injury law firm in New York. Frankly, working as a mailroom clerk paid much less than an entry legal assistant or entry-level paralegal, which were the positions I initially sought. Since I had my bachelor's degree, I was also quite overqualified for the mail clerk position. Nonetheless, I decided to make the best of the opportunity. Though my first job out of university was a low-paying position, the fact that I got to work in a law firm was an exciting opportunity.

Law school was only a few months away, and I decided to be very intentional with my time at the firm. In essence, I decided to absorb as much knowledge as possible about the legal industry that I hoped I would one day be a part of. I showed up to work early and often left late. As I did so, I began to build connections with the attorneys and legal staff and shared my intention to attend law school the following year. My pattern of constantly giving a helping hand to whatever was needed by the attorneys influenced the manager's decision to create a legal assistant position for me. After three months of going above the call of my mailroom clerk duties, I began working as a legal assistant, which also meant a better salary. In retrospect, I desired a better position, but none was available, so I simply decided to make the best of the situation. My strong work ethic did not go unnoticed, influencing my employers to create a better-paying position for me.

I enjoyed working as a legal assistant so much that I briefly contemplated continuing in the legal support staff position long-term and perhaps becoming a paralegal. This idea was short-lived. When I shared my change of career idea with a firm's managing partner, he told me upfront that I had too much greatness and encouraged me that I could go farther than a paralegal. The partner's confidence that I would go on to do great things as an attorney was a refreshing reminder not to settle for anything less than the best.

While working as a legal assistant, the pastor at the church I attended in Brooklyn, New York, encouraged me to see if I could secure any scholarships to attend law school in New York. After applying to a handful of law schools in New York, the Maurice A. Deane School of Law at Hofstra University in Hempstead offered me a partial scholarship, and I accepted. After working on OPT for a year, I started Hofstra Law School in Hempstead, New York, while Colliet commenced her law studies at University of Florida Levin School of Law in Florida. My sisters and I were studying in different locations for the first time. It took some time for us to adjust, but we did and remained in communication with each other.

Our graduate school experience differed greatly from our undergraduate experience. First, our undergraduate school was a relatively small college with a predominantly black student population, while the law schools that Colliet and I attended were larger institutions with a predominantly white student body. Second, law and medical schools generally have more specialized courses, and the academic competitiveness among students is intense. Third, our undergraduate scholarships essentially covered our entire tuition and room and board, compared to law and medical schools, where we had to figure out how we would pay for the remaining tuition and room and board expenses. In other words, my sisters and I had significantly more expenses to pay to obtain our graduate degrees.

As I shared earlier, Colleen eventually secured a loan to cover her medical school tuition. Colliet likewise secured a private loan to cover the remaining tuition balance that her scholarship did not cover. Colleen and Colliet's tuition fees were covered, but their student housing rent was not. It was indeed exhausting managing demanding coursework and having to figure out how one's rent would be paid. With the threat of eviction constantly lurking, Colleen and Colliet had to live by faith. However, as mentioned in the Bible, faith without works is dead (see James 2:26), so in addition to faith, they needed to work. Colleen's busy academic schedule made securing employment while studying extremely difficult, so she worked her faith by constantly reaching out to different folks for assistance with her rent. In some way, Colleen's way of life was that of a personal GoFundMe account because she raised money for her rent every month by asking for financial donations. It was a tiring and stressful ordeal.

One day, Colleen broke down in tears while explaining to our mother how mentally and emotionally draining it was not knowing how her rent would be paid. It broke our mother's heart to see Colleen struggle like this. After a year of enduring this difficult ordeal, a relative from England heard of Colleen's situation and miraculously offered to pay her rent while she studied at RSUM. This was a tremendous blessing for Colleen.

Like Colleen, who was unable to work while studying, Colliet and I could not obtain part-time employment at our respective law schools until we became second-year students. This meant that Colliet and I had to rely on the financial assistance of others to cover our monthly rent. Because New York is one of the most expensive states to live in and study, my tuition and student housing were twice as expensive as Colliet's Florida law school tuition and student housing. Frankly, I was facing a financial plight because I started my first semester of law school without knowing how to pay my school fees. Though I was at a financial crossroads, I decided not to borrow any traditional loans. At the time, my law school offered payment plans to help students who could not make a lump sum payment, and I decided to enroll in the program. While grappling with threats of being evicted from my law school and dorm room, Alton and Melony Samuels, the overseers at the church I attended in Brooklyn, New York, reached out their hands to me and pulled me out of my financial woes. Though I was practically a stranger to them then, they decided to help cover my first year of law school fees. They also graciously offered to help Colliet with her monthly rent, so we were both saved from law school and student housing eviction.

I lessened my law school expenses during my second and third years by moving in with my older sister, who lived in Brooklyn, New York. I had to hunt for a paid summer internship to pay for the second and third years of law school. When I think about how I secured paid employment while studying law, I think about the importance of working smart and hard. Working hard is diligently optimizing your time to ensure you perform well in your study. Working smart is making strategic decisions that take you to the next level.

When I was in my first year of law school, I had to work hard, and I had to work smart. I had law school expenses that my scholarship did not cover, and I wanted to avoid taking out any traditional loans. I knew I needed a well-paying summer job to help me with my law school expenses, so I intentionally did not apply for any unpaid summer internships. Finding a paid summer internship as an international student was extremely challenging because many required United States citizenship or permanent residency. As an international student, I felt as though I was at the bottom of the barrel regarding the hiring hierarchy. OPT authorized me to work, but finding an employer willing to pay me to work was an uphill battle. Eventually, I found a paid internship program that accepted international students, and I applied. This paid internship was through the New York City Diversity Bar Fellowship. This program is essentially a pipeline program to help law school students from underrepresented populations access New York's leading law firms and corporate/government law departments. Ironically, as an undergraduate student, the paid internship I secured was also through a pipeline program, the Ronald H. Brown Pre-Law Program, which helps underrepresented students gain admission to law school and work experience in the legal field.

The money I earned as a summer associate at a leading New York law firm was not enough to cover my entire tuition. I must say, however, that a substantial portion of my law school expenses was covered through working on OPT during the summers of my first and second summer of law school. I also used any tax reimbursements I received to cover my tuition. This shows the incredible opportunity that OPT affords international students. Despite using OPT to work to help pay for law school, I was still facing a deficit to cover my entire law school tuition.

There is a saying that a closed mouth does not get fed, which is very true. In our plight to cross the finish line to become the doctor and lawyers my sisters and I aspired to be, we had to reach out to others to help cover our remaining expenses. We reached out to family members living abroad, our church community, and folks in corporate Jamaica. With the outpour of financial assistance that we received, I graduated with my juris doctorate from Hofstra Law School and passed the New York Bar exam. Colliet graduated with her juris doctorate from UF Levin School of Law and passed the Florida Bar exam. Colliet also completed the Norman Manley six-month program and is licensed to practice law in Jamaica. Colleen graduated from Ross School of Medicine and is a medical doctor.

Today, the Bramwell triplet from Tivoli Gardens are living their dream as two lawyers and a doctor.

Part II
The Aspiring F-1 Student

Chapter VI

The Top-Tier Student

If you are a high schooler desiring to attend college or university in the United States on a scholarship, you must pay keen attention to your academics. Whether you attend a traditional or non-traditional high school is of no significance. All that matters is how you spend your time at school. There is no room for idleness because there is a limited timeframe in which you must accomplish your academic goals.

My sisters and I began our CSEC journey in grade 9. By doing so, we lessened the number of subjects we needed to sit in grade 11. Grade 9 is a great trial opportunity to take a CSEC exam. If your high school allows students to take a CSEC exam before grade 11, I recommend taking at least one CSEC subject between grades 9 and 10. This subject can be any subject of your choice, but keep in mind that you will be responsible for mastering the subject outside of your regular classes. I recommend a subject that is part of your regular classes. By doing this, you will already have the necessary textbooks and course materials needed to prepare for the exam, and a grade teacher who you can easily ask questions.

You should choose a subject tailored to your capabilities, which requires candid introspection. Social studies was a great selection for us because it was being taught in our regular classes, and we were aware that we were not prepared to take on any of the more complex subjects, such as mathematics. The topics covered in social studies were much more relatable than trigonometry. Since this will be your first time taking a CSEC subject and you still have two more years to do additional CSEC subjects, select a relatable and manageable subject.

In addition to taking at least one CSEC subject in grade 9, I recommend participating in extracurricular leadership activities. When applying for college admissions in the United States, you will have to write a college admission essay known as a personal statement. This essay needs to demonstrate that you are a top-tier student who deserves both an acceptance and a scholarship. Top-tier students are well-rounded students who maintain excellent grades while engaging in extracurricular leadership activities. If you are not in a club or group, now is the time to join one that aligns with your interests and goals.

Your participation in various school activities builds character and will help you draft a good personal statement when the time comes. At Tivoli Gardens High School, we were active members of the Peer Educators Club for over two years. Colleen and I were prefects, while Colliet was the school's Deputy Head Girl and later Head Girl. Through the Peer Educators Club, we gave back to our high school and our inner-city community. Together, we hosted educational forums, sponsored talent shows, and collected food items to distribute to the elderly at our community nursing home. We had no idea how much these activities would help to differentiate us from our peers. These activities, coupled with our strong academic grades, paved the way for us to obtain our scholarships to study in the United States. If you want to attend college or university in the United States on a scholarship, you must differentiate yourself by becoming a top-tier student.

Many low-income students in Jamaica and the Caribbean have socio-economic challenges. If you are reading this book, your financial circumstances do not differentiate you or your trajectory. There are many people with similar stories. Your personal challenge is inconsequential in getting a scholarship. Otherwise, more students would be attending college on scholarships. What compels United States college or university admissions boards to give you a scholarship is demonstrating to them how you have succeeded despite your circumstances. Doing the bare minimum to graduate high school is different from succeeding. Success in high school means excelling in your academics and extracurricular activities. Does that mean you must get an A in every subject? Not at all. We did not get an A in every subject. You must, however, demonstrate that you have maintained a strong academic grade despite disappointing events.

Recall, Colliet and I initially failed CSEC mathematics. Aside from being embarrassed, we had a goal of going to college on a scholarship, and we had to buckle down and sit the exam again. Failure was unacceptable, so we devised a strategy to ensure we performed well when we retook the exam. On the second attempt at the CSEC mathematics, we found a knowledgeable upper-level student from our community and pleaded with him to help us prepare for the exam. As usual, we had no money to pay for a private tutor, but knowing that failure was unacceptable, we searched aggressively for someone willing to assist us for free, and, fortunately, we eventually found someone. Because we could not pay, we worked on his time, which meant we ensured we were also available whenever he was available. We retook the exam and got grades II and III, respectively. Note that neither of us got a grade I in mathematics, but in the aggregate, we had so many other CSEC subjects with grades I and II that we could still demonstrate strong academic success.

If you can get a grade I in every CSEC subject you take in grade 11, then you should absolutely do so. From a practical perspective, this will only be the case for some. This does not mean that attending college or university in the United States on a scholarship is beyond your reach. Instead, like my sisters and I, you need to start taking CSEC subjects incrementally (if your school allows you to). If you recall, my classmate's scholarship opportunity was forfeited because her CSEC grades were unsatisfactory. My classmate's exact words when she found out she could not continue with the scholarship program was that she *"wished someone had told her earlier that this opportunity would present itself."* Had she known, she would have taken her academics more seriously. This tragedy taught me the importance of academic readiness. Academic readiness means ensuring that your academic grades reflect that you are a diligent student, and that you can take advantage of scholastic opportunities whenever they present themselves. Regardless of your high school and community, if you commit early to working hard, you can attend a college or university in the United States on scholarships.

Although you do not need a grade I in every CSEC subject, a grade I in most of your CSEC subjects is ideal. When you apply for college in the United States, you want to ensure your CSEC grades are a mixture of grades I and II in the aggregate. To do this, you need to be practical about the likelihood of receiving a passing grade on all your CSEC exams in grade 11. Remember that when I speak of passing, I mean receiving a grade I or II in all the subjects that you sit. I recommend taking at least eight CSEC subjects throughout your tenure at high school. Mathematics and English language are non-negotiable subjects and must be included in your selection. Additionally, most colleges and universities in the United States expect you to have subjects in natural science, i.e., biology, chemistry, or physics; social science, i.e., social studies, geography, or Caribbean history; and a foreign language, i.e., French or Spanish. As a top-tier student wishing to study in the United States, you must secure a subject in each category.

Once you have registered for your chosen CSEC exam, you must manage your time wisely. Proper time management is not optional. It is mandatory if you want to achieve your goals. Remember, your most valuable asset in high school is time management. Please use it wisely. By grade 9, you should engage in extracurricular leadership activities, keep up with your regular coursework, and study for your CSEC exam. Balancing schoolwork, extracurricular activities, and preparing for a CSEC exam will be tiring. If you do not have anyone to guide you through the CSEC materials, then you will have an additional burden of self-mastery.

Irrespective of the CSEC subject you select, you need to understand that you are deciding to sit an exam earlier than you need to. Generally, the curriculums for the various CSEC subjects are designed to cover the required course materials over a certain period and thereby prepare students to sit their respective exams in grade 11. Take, for example, the CSEC subject Caribbean History. All the necessary historical course materials a student sitting for the exam needs to acquire for sufficient knowledge are usually not covered in one academic year. Instead, as students transition from one grade to the next, the curriculum is designed such that, over time, students build a rich repository of all the historical information that the exam will test for in grade 11. Most Caribbean high school students will follow this timeline and only take CSEC exams in grade 11. However, this timeline can become problematic for low-income high school students looking to attend college or university in the United States.

How likely are you to score high on all your CSEC subjects if you wait until grade 11? If you can commit to the work, you could likely pass all your subjects. But merely passing is different from receiving those high scores you need to help you obtain a United States college scholarship. You can receive a grade III on a CSEC exam, demonstrating satisfactory standard passing performance. However, when seeking an academic scholarship from a college or university in the United States, you will need more than the standard performance on an exam to obtain a full scholarship. Taking your CSEC exams from grade 9 will give you the requisite experience and room to make mistakes and recover. Granted, this means that you will have less time to learn all the necessary course materials for the CSEC subjects you choose to do before grade 11. In taking CSEC subjects that are manageable and relatable, you will be solely responsible for learning course materials beyond what your teacher may cover in grade 9. Although this is different from the traditional way students take CSECs, it is very doable, but only if you are willing to do the work.

There is a saying that your network is your net worth, which rings true even in high school. Grade 9 is the opportune time to seek out students and teachers who can help you along your CSEC readiness journey—teachers who truly care about their students often go the extra mile to help students who consistently show they want to succeed academically. Consider joining a study group if serious-minded students in upper-level classes are sitting the same CSEC exam you are taking. If one is unavailable, you can take the initiative to create one. All you need is to find one dedicated upper-level student willing to help you, which may take some convincing. The upper-level student can be the student-teacher, and they can practice the concepts with you as they are learning them. One of the best ways to test whether you truly understand a subject is when you can teach it to someone else. For inner-city students like my sisters and me, who never had any money to pay for extra lessons or private tutors, you must make a way even when there seems to be no way. Remember, failure is unacceptable.

In addition to seeking guidance from teachers and peers, the curriculum and past exam papers will become your best friend as you prepare for your CSEC exam. Past exam papers provide the exam's objective, format, and patterns that consistently show up.

With all the help you may get from teachers and upper-level students, the heavy lifting of the coursework will still be on your shoulders. No one can do the work for you. Therefore, you must make time to comb through the materials independently. This will likely mean waking up in the middle of the night to study or spending your weekends at school to learn the subject. Even if you are the only person in your grade 9 class sitting a CSEC exam, you cannot allow this to deter you. Make sure you comb through your respective textbooks and all the corresponding quizzes. To facilitate your retention of the materials, practice taking notes as you review the chapters. By doing this, you are forcing yourself to engage in the materials, which is very helpful, especially during those late nights of studying when you are fighting the urge to sleep. As you take notes, you will likely feel like you are taking longer to complete the textbook chapters. This is true, but it is much better to go slower, knowing you retain the information.

In addition to taking notes, you must review every question you got wrong and understand why you did. By dissecting your answer choices, you can understand why they are incorrect compared to the other choices, which will be particularly important for multiple-choice questions.

If you follow these recommendations, at the start of grade 10, you should be well ahead of your peers, with at least one CSEC subject successfully secured. If you did not receive a grade I or II in the CSEC subject you took in grade 9, there is no need to retake the exam unless you failed. However, you will need to assess why you did not score higher on the exam. You can identify and eliminate the issues you believe affected your score and prevent them from reoccurring. Grade 10 is a continuation of the steps you took in grade 9. You improve where necessary, replicate the study habits you developed in grade 9, and continue your extracurricular activities. Like grade 9, you must register for another CSEC subject by October or November. As I mentioned, choose a subject taught in your regular classes. By this time, you will be familiar with the CSEC exam model and have a general understanding of what to expect, regardless of the subject you choose to take in grade 10. While your friends attend various social events, you will not have the pleasure of accompanying them. Your time should be spent mastering your CSEC subject, which you must sit in May or June.

Understanding how much of your academic readiness depends on you is essential. For most of you reading this book, like my sisters and I, paying for private lessons or a private tutor is not within your family's budget. No one is continuously watching over your shoulder to ensure you do the work required, and if you need that type of reinforcement, then this book is not for you. You must push yourself even when no one is there cheering you on. You must burn the midnight lamp and learn the materials. We sat on the cold concrete floor of our kitchen and living room, and it was uncomfortable, but it helped to keep us awake at night when we needed to study. This is hard work, but it will be worth it. You need to finish grade 10 strong, stronger than how you finished grade 9. When you sit your CSEC exam, you need to be confident you gave it your all to ensure the best result possible.

Before you know it, you will be in grade 11, and beast-mode needs to be fully activated. If you follow my recommendation, you should have a minimum of two CSEC subjects secured. At the onset of grade 11, only a few students will be able to say this. Every day of your grade 11 is important, and you cannot afford to spend your time on unfruitful activities. Unlike grade 9 and grade 10, you need to take multiple CSEC subjects in the same academic year. This can seem overwhelming, especially since you will take more complex subjects. There is no need to fear because, at this point, you should be aware of what you need to do. By taking CSEC subjects incrementally, you developed a routine of burning the midnight lamp amid all your regular coursework and extracurricular activities. Repeat the steps that you have taken.

Aside from the non-negotiable CSEC subjects (Mathematics, English Language, a natural science subject, a social science subject, and a foreign language), you are free to select those subjects that align with your academic interest and career aspirations. I urge you not to sit for vocational examinations such as those offered through the City and Guilds. City and Guilds primarily focus on vocational education and are intended to prepare students for the working world. If you want to attend college in the United States, your focus should be on CSEC subjects, and you have several subjects to choose from.

If you decide to sit eight CSEC subjects incrementally, as I recommend, by grade 11, you only need to do six subjects (assuming you do two subjects between grades 9 and 10). If you opt to do three CSEC subjects between grade 9 and grade 10 (like I did), you only need to sit five subjects in grade 11. Having fewer subjects to take in grade 11, without reducing the total number of subjects you need in the aggregate, means that you can devote more time to the other complex subjects. Grade 11 is a critical period in your CSEC journey. Any mistake you make will cost you money and time. Regardless of the CSEC subject you are taking in grade 11, your aim is to score high on the exam. You need to devote adequate time to mastering the nooks and crannies of the subjects. This does not guarantee you will receive a grade I in every subject, but you will be consumed with the particulars of the various CSEC subjects and positioned to score well on the exams. This scenario epitomizes academic readiness. By aggressively tackling your academics, you are positioning yourself not to have any regrets.

As you strive for academic success, unforeseen life events will occur. It is easy to say you should not allow this to distract you in your pursuit of academic readiness, but those words are not helpful when disturbing events such as the loss of a parent occurs, and your heart feels completely shattered, leaving you in a debilitating state. Studying during such a difficult period is no easy task, and our experience can attest to this. It is truly a test of one's ability to persevere, and frankly speaking, I cannot tell you that you should ignore your pain. That is unhealthy, especially when striving to be a top-tier student. If an uncontrollable and unforeseen situation arises, it does not mean you quit your studies. Adjust accordingly, but please do not give up hope and completely pull the brakes on your academic goals. Our father died in the middle of an exam period, and we were utterly devastated. We attempted to study for our exams, and as we read our textbook, we had to wipe tears from our eyes continuously. Though our textbook got wet from our tears that seemed like they would never end, we continued our studies. Our teachers empathized with our struggles and permitted us to be excused from our internal exam.

Unfortunately, the CSEC exams are not very forgiving of unforeseen life events. If a situation arises that would seemingly justify your reasons for not being motivated to continue striving for high grades, it is very unlikely that the examiners will allow you to take the exam when it is more accommodating to you. I urge students in this position to view their CSEC exams from a much broader perspective. Your CSEC subjects are valuable because you need them to get to the next level in life: college. In finding the strength to continue with your studies, you are honoring your dreams and aspirations of a better life. In the case of losing someone you loved, you are also honoring that deceased person because they would likely have wanted you to continue succeeding academically and in life in general. Therefore, should an unforeseen event occur during grade 11, the most critical year of high school, I say to you, push forward—on days when you cannot, take a break and go at it again the next day. You will eventually reap the reward of your diligent work. A top-tier student rests when they must and does not quit despite the challenges that come their way.

In addition to unforeseen life events, there is also the possibility that you may fail a CSEC subject. This is an undesirable outcome, but since I want to be practical, let us discuss the strategy that should be implemented if this happens. If you fail a non-negotiable CSEC subject, especially Mathematics or English Language, you should retake the exam administered in February of the upcoming year. Retaking the CSEC exam and receiving a grade III on the exam is much better than choosing not to redo the exam. On this academic journey, failure is unacceptable. You must retake and pass the CSEC exam you failed. If the CSEC exam you failed is a particularly weak subject, I recommend finding a tutor or taking private lessons. Low-income students will need additional help but lack the resources to pay. We are prime examples, but we did not let that hinder us from retaking and passing our CSEC exam. For those students who must retake an exam, I implore you to get as many past CSEC exam papers on the subject as possible. This is an excellent starting point. Review the past papers thoroughly. Do not be afraid to seek help from your high school, even if you are no longer a student.

Colleen sought assistance from our high school after she graduated. She realized she needed to take the Chemistry CSEC exam because she wanted to study pre-med in college. As usual, our mother could not afford to pay for Colleen to do private chemistry lessons. Refusing to accept defeat, Colleen pleaded with our high school principal to be allowed to sit in the grade 11 chemistry classes. Our principal agreed on the condition that Colleen wore her uniform whenever she attended classes. Folks at school and in our neighborhood were confused and shocked when they saw Colleen walking to school in her uniform, especially since we had just graduated high school a few months prior. Imagine the gossip that stirred when people realized one of the Bramwell Triplets, a top-tier student, was repeating high school! On the other hand, Colleen was relentless in her decision to sit the chemistry CSEC exam, and the opinions of others would not sway her otherwise. She did what she needed to do and passed her chemistry CSEC exam. High schoolers who must retake any CSEC exam need to be relentless in their pursuit like Colleen. Even if you do not receive a high score when you retake the exam, if it is a passing score, you will be okay if, in the aggregate, you completed grade 9 to grade 11 with a healthy mixture of your CSEC subjects in grade I or II.

Jamaica's Ministry of Education announced the implementation of a seven-year high school program known as the New Sixth Form Pathways. As of September 2022, high schoolers are required to complete seven years of high school. Therefore, students who complete grade 11 must transition to grades 12 and 13. I urge Jamaican and Caribbean students interested in studying in the United States who must attend Sixth Form to sit the Caribbean Advance Proficiency Examinations (i.e., CAPE). In most cases, satisfactory CAPE results can be applied as college credits, enabling you to complete college or university in less than the typical four-year requirement.

Under Jamaica's Ministry of Education 2021 guidelines regarding the New Sixth Form Program, students can only sit for CAPE if they have a minimum of five CSEC subjects, including Mathematics or English Language. Students who approach CSECs in the manner I have suggested should not have any issues meeting these requirements since I have reiterated the need for Mathematics and English language as non-negotiable CSEC subjects, as well as the need to sit for at least eight CSEC subjects by the end of grade 11. When selecting your CAPE subjects, ensure that you continue picking subjects that United States colleges and universities look for (i.e., Mathematics, English Language, Natural Science, Social Science, and a foreign language). During Sixth Form, you must maintain your commitment to being academically prepared to take advantage of the educational opportunities that lie ahead. The exam format may change since you are no longer taking CSEC subjects, but the foundational principle of academic excellence still applies.

Chapter VII

SAT Self-Guided Studier

Suppose you are from a low-income family and desire to attend university or college in the United States on scholarships without taking any loans. In that case, you must position yourself to excel academically. The higher you score on the Scholastic Aptitude Test (i.e., SAT), which is a standardized test used by most colleges and universities in the United States to make admission decisions, the more likely you are to obtain scholarships. Therefore, the SAT is crucial to a United States college application. Most colleges and universities in the United States also accept the American College Test (i.e., ACT). However, this book only covers the SAT.

When we took the SAT in 2011, the test consisted of three main sections: critical reading, writing and essay, and math. Each section was scored out of 800; the highest score a person could receive was 2400. In 2016, the College Board, a not-for-profit organization in the United States authorized to design the SAT, implemented several changes, including changes to the section structure, length of the test, score range, total number of questions, and scoring policy. Under this revised SAT structure, the reading and writing sections have been combined into one section titled 'Evidence-Based Reading and Writing' along with an optional essay section. A student's maximum score under the revised SAT is 1600, with each section scored out of

800. In July 2021, the College Board decided to discontinue the optional essay writing component, and the overall time allotted to take the exam is now three hours. When we took the SAT in 2011, we lost a quarter point for each incorrect answer selection. Luckily, the revised SAT no longer penalizes students for incorrect answer selections.

The SAT is generally administered in March, May, June, August, October, November, and December. There are currently seven SAT test locations in Jamaica (American International School of Kingston, Belair Secondary School, Campion College, Dinthill Technical School, Mount Alvernia High School, St Andrew High School for Girls, and The Priory School). To register online for the SAT, you need to create an account via the College Board website and pay the applicable registration fee which is currently US$60.00. However, the SAT registration fee may vary depending on when you take the exam. To perform well on the SAT, it is crucial that you understand the format of the test, which has 154 multiple-choice questions. The evidence-based reading and writing section of the test is divided into two parts, one for Reading, and the other for Writing and Language. There are 52 multiple-choice questions in the Reading section covering passages relating to history and social studies, sciences, and United States and world literature. There are 44 multiple-choice questions in the Writing and Language section based on nonfictional passages. There are 54 multiple-choice questions in the Math section. You can use a calculator during the first 25 minutes of the math section. After a short break, you will likely move on to the final 55-minute section for math, but you are not allowed to use a calculator during this section.

Now that you understand how important the SAT score is, you must devote as much time as possible preparing for this important exam. Additionally, you will need to consider whether your family can afford to pay for you to take private SAT prep courses. Private SAT prep courses are helpful if you are looking to attend college in the United States, and if your family can pay for you to take a SAT prep course, then I recommend you do so since they provide valuable services as you embark on your United States college admission process. Private SAT prep courses can be quite expensive for the average Jamaican and Caribbean household, and are often not a feasible option for many low-income youths. Growing up in Tivoli Gardens, we knew our mother could not afford private SAT prep courses. Fortunately, the Rotary Club scholarship paid for our SAT prep expenses at Versan Educational Services.

Unfortunately, not every low-income Caribbean student will find a sponsor willing to pay for them to do private SAT prep courses. As a low-income student, the thought of studying for the SAT can be daunting, overwhelming, and expensive, especially if you lack the financial resources to take a private SAT prep course. I see you, and I hear you. But, guess what? The hefty price tag attached to a missed opportunity is too expensive, and you cannot allow any barriers to stop you from pursuing your dreams. Given that one's SAT score is a decisive factor, and private SAT prep courses are expensive, low-income Caribbean students need more affordable SAT prep options. Like my father told me, you are a star that shines no matter what. As a low-income Caribbean student, you must be amenable in your approach without losing sight of the end goal. Remember, you can attend college or university in the United States on a scholarship, regardless of your background.

For low-income Jamaican and Caribbean students who cannot afford to pay an average of US$1,000.00 (or more) for SAT courses through private companies, I recommend checking with your teachers at your high school to see if they, or someone they know, offers SAT classes. These classes are often much cheaper than paying for courses through private companies because they typically focus solely on SAT prep. They often do not provide guidance with gathering the necessary college admission materials, for example, preparing one's personal statement that the United States colleges require for admission. SAT prep courses via private companies provide comprehensive guidance throughout your United States college admission process. If you pay for private SAT prep courses, they will generally assist you with SAT prep, college applications (including your personal statements), and the student visa process.

Suppose the teachers at your high school do not offer SAT courses, and you cannot pay for private courses or a tutor. In that case, you have much more work to do since you cannot pay for someone with the expertise to guide you through the many nuances of the SAT exam and the United States college admission process. You will have to self-study for the SAT. Do not be disappointed. You are not the first or the last student to find themselves in this position. There are so many similarly situated students who have strong CSEC and CAPE grades. However, they simply do not have the money these private SAT prep companies require before accepting students into their programs. If you are one of those students who will have to self-study for the SAT, now is the time to tighten your belt and prepare for the arduous journey ahead.

Remember what I have reiterated in the previous chapters: success is where preparation meets opportunity. You may lack money, but you do not lack time. Time is your currency! It is important that you understand what this means. When it comes to time, everyone on the planet gets the same 24 hours per day. The same time management principles you must apply in high school to graduate with strong CSEC (and CAPE grades, if applicable) will apply as you focus on scoring high on the SAT. Because the SAT is not part of Caribbean high school curriculums, you may be at a disadvantage, and this is one of the reasons that those who can afford to pay approximately US$1,000.00 (or more) for someone to teach them how to increase their score on the exam do so.

For many low-income Caribbean students, the SAT will be an incredibly challenging exam, and students need to devote a lot of time to learning the granularity of the SAT and practice increasing their scores as much as possible. Jamaican and Caribbean students, particularly students from low-income households who have to self-study for the SAT exam, may consider taking a year off (i.e., a gap year) after graduating high school before starting college in the United States. In other words, you should start college the year after your high school graduation. For students who automatically gasped (and shook their heads in disagreement), at least hear my rationale for suggesting this option. First, you may need to retake and pass a CSEC or Cape exam that you failed (especially if it is a non-negotiable subject) prior to starting college in the United States. Second, you need to give keen attention to your SAT studies (including retaking the exam if necessary). It is particularly helpful to do so without the hassle of managing other competing demands such as classwork or extracurricular activities. Third, you need to focus on compiling a strong college application, including drafting your personal statement.

We took a gap year after graduating high school (grade 11, we did not go to sixth form). It was indeed an invaluable opportunity to focus solely on SAT prep and college applications. During our gap year, Colliet and I retook and passed CSEC mathematics, which we had initially failed. A gap year is essentially an opportunity to improve your SAT score and enhance your college application. If, at the time of reading this book, you are in your final year of high school (i.e., grade 11, if you choose not to go to sixth form; or lower sixth form (grade 12), if you choose not to go to upper sixth form; or upper sixth form (grade 13), if both grade 12 and grade 13 are mandatory) and you have to self-study for the SAT, you need to use the months after graduation to study for the SAT and take the exam by October. If you are unhappy with your score, you can retake the exam in November or December of that year. This means you will not follow the traditional approach of taking the SAT while in high school and applying for college in the United States before graduation.

Alternatively, if you want to follow the traditional approach of starting college right after graduating high school, and you have to self-study for the SAT, I recommend using the summer months immediately before starting your final year in high school to begin studying for the SAT. You should then take the SAT exam by October of the first semester of your final year in high school. If you are unhappy with your SAT score, you can retake the exam in November or December of that year. United States college and university applications are usually due between November and February of the college or university entrance year, and you are likely to get a response from schools in March or April. It is important to know that December's score is your last opportunity to take the SAT and still meet the January or February application deadline most United States colleges and universities have in place. Regardless of when you decide to take the SAT, you must ensure that you take the exam well before the United States college or university application deadlines, which will vary depending on the school you apply to.

Most colleges and universities in the United States have implemented a SAT score choice whereby students can submit the SAT score they want the school to see. For example, if you took the SAT three times, you don't have to send all three score reports to the college or university you applied to. Instead, you can choose which test score you would like to send. Let's say you took the SAT in October, November, and December and scored your best on the December tests. By using score choice, you only need to submit the December test results. The college or university you apply to will not see how you scored on the October or November tests.

Additionally, most colleges and universities in the United States superscore the SAT. By using superscore, colleges and universities consider your highest section scores across multiple test dates. For example, if you took the SAT in October, November, and December, a school that allows you to superscore would pull your highest score from each section of the test to derive your superscore. Let's say your October math score of 600 was the highest of the three tests, and your December Evidence-Based Reading and Writing score of 650 was the highest of the three tests. By taking your best scores from the different test sections, your superscore would be 1250. Not all colleges and universities in the United States allow superscore or score choice, so it is important to check the school's admission page to learn about its testing policies.

As a self-guided SAT student, you have opted for the least expensive means of exam preparation and potentially the most challenging approach. Without guidance from a SAT tutor/teacher-led SAT class, you will likely wonder how to prioritize the areas you should study. Do not panic. On this self-study journey, you must learn to utilize all the available and affordable resources. Before studying for the SAT, I recommend researching (i.e., reviewing articles, blog posts, YouTube videos, etc.) how other students successfully self-studied for the SAT. Essentially, you are looking for SAT book recommendations and helpful study plans from someone in a similar situation (i.e., a former SAT self-study student). You also need to research budget-friendly SAT prep resources and make the best use of them. Take, for example, Khan Academy, a renowned not-for-profit organization that partnered with the makers of the SAT exam College Board, to create a free SAT prep program. At the time of writing this book, Khan Academy did not offer any live SAT online courses where students could connect with an instructor. However, the prep program provides unlimited diagnostic quizzes, hundreds of practice questions, and multiple free online and downloadable full-length practice tests.

To be familiar with the SAT format, you must practice questions that are structured similarly to the SAT exam. It is not helpful to practice with questions that are harder or easier than the actual SAT exam. Official SAT practice questions and tests published by the College Board (and available through Khan Academy) represent what you will see on the test. One of the amazing features that Khan Academy provides is the ability for students to connect their college board account to the prep program. For students who take official SAT practice test, connecting your college board account allows Khan Academy to analyze your performance on previous SAT practice exams and recommend customized practice questions and explanatory videos that you should focus on to see improvements in your SAT performance. This free resource is a great tool to have in your SAT prep arsenal.

You will need at least one highly rated SAT prep book on the SAT self-guided journey. Unfortunately, not all SAT prep books are created equally. You must conduct your research to identify SAT book(s) that are consistently ranked high amongst SAT takers. Generally, the SAT book(s) you select should include a thorough review of the topics on the SAT or a specific SAT section, test-taking tips and strategies, realistic SAT practice questions and tests, and detailed answer explanations. When the time comes to begin studying for the SAT, you want to hit the ground running, and you cannot do so without your SAT book(s). Therefore, you need to get them well before commencing your SAT studies, even as early as the summer before you plan to study (i.e., one year ahead of your SAT study date).

Once you have your SAT book(s), and the time comes for you to begin your SAT prep, the very first thing you must do (even before you read any of your SAT books) is to take a mock SAT exam (i.e., a diagnostic test, and you can use one of the free SAT practice tests from the College Board website) under similar test-like conditions. You cannot ignore this point. To understand the areas of the SAT that you are weak or strong in, you need to take a mock SAT exam that gives you an accurate baseline. This baseline score is your starting point because it will tell you where you currently score on the SAT. You do not need to prepare; you just need to take the test under the same test-like conditions. This means you cannot start the test and pause whenever you want. You also cannot go to the bathroom whenever you want during the test. You must do the test under similar test conditions, and it is your responsibility to ensure this happens. To facilitate this, ensure that you take the test in a quiet environment, and given that SAT exams are usually administered on a Saturday, aim to take the test at the time that the test is usually administered, between 8:30 am and 9:00 am.

After you have completed your mock SAT exam and have your baseline score, your goal is to understand why you missed what you missed and learn strategies and concepts that will help you improve your SAT score. As a self-guided SAT student, you must create an effective study plan. An effective study plan should include realistic and specific actionable items to be completed by your official SAT test date. In high school, a curriculum usually outlines the topics a teacher would cover throughout the academic year. One of the most helpful things about a curriculum is the planned sequence of provided topics. Think of your self-guided SAT plan as your personal planned sequence of actionable goals. Given that this is your plan, there is flexibility for you to move certain topics around, depending on the amount of time you must prepare for the exam. To do well on the SAT by the self-study method, you need to have an elevated level of self-discipline. This trait is non-negotiable. Stick with your study plan, and do not give up. If you plan to complete a set number of practice questions and review the corresponding answer explanations for a given day, you must complete this task. On this self-study journey, please do not try to cheat yourself by procrastinating. There is no easy way out. It would be best if you put in the work to increase your baseline SAT score as much as possible.

As a self-guided SAT student, consistency is crucial for your success. If you can find a library to study, then please do so. We did not have the bus fare to go to the library daily while studying for the SAT, so we often studied at home. Our home was usually quiet throughout the day since everyone else was at work. However, we lived in the inner-city, and it was not unusual for loud music to play on the street at any hour of the day. Men playing dominoes and hitting the board heavily each time was also the norm. Our inner-city community was usually noisy, but it was never an excuse not to get our studies done. Likewise, your environment is not an excuse either. To increase your SAT score (based on your mock SAT result), I strongly urge students to ensure they have balanced meals and are getting adequate rest. The SAT is not a sprint. It is a marathon. This means that you must refrain from cramming for this exam. Rather, you need to put in time (consistently) and diligently prepare for this exam.

Every SAT student should have a goal score. This is the score you must have to be admitted to the United States college or university you apply to. In 2019, the College Board indicated that the average SAT score was 1050, which is acceptable for admissions at most colleges. Our SAT scores were within the range necessary to be considered for admission. However, these scores were not within the range needed to increase our likelihood of attending college in the United States on full scholarships. We had to be very intentional with the colleges we applied to increase the likelihood of obtaining the most scholarship possible. As you continue studying for the SAT and take practice SAT tests, you will begin to see the score range you are within. Based on your average SAT scores from your practice exams, you can begin to look at the United States colleges and universities that you have a good chance of being admitted to. But let's be realistic; you are not putting in all this work just to get admitted; you also need as many scholarships as possible. Thus, regardless of the colleges you apply to, you should aim for colleges where your score is considered competitive. For example, a 1350 SAT score makes your college application more competitive because it places you in the top 10% of SAT takers. A competitive SAT score means more scholarships for you. Therefore, you will be in a particularly good position if your SAT score is a goal score (i.e., the score needed for admission depending on the colleges you apply to) and a competitive score (i.e., the score needed to be considered for scholarship awards).

As you work towards increasing your SAT score, frustration will likely creep in if you do not see your baseline score increase to the desired score needed to be considered for scholarship awards. This is quite a common issue amongst SAT test takers, even those taking private SAT prep courses. Significant SAT improvement can happen, but it does not happen easily, especially if you are going to self-study for the SAT. Because I know that this is a prevalent issue, and I also know that failure is not an option, I want to discuss options for those students who do not see a significant increase in their SAT score when they compare it to their baseline score (unless your baseline score was already a very competitive score, in which case, job well done).

If, after assiduously preparing for the SAT, you do not see a significant increase in your SAT score, I recommend being very strategic in your college selection by applying to colleges where your SAT score puts you in a position where the colleges will offer you some money. In other words, your SAT score is a compass that should guide you in your college selection. Admittedly, there are other things that matter on your journey to gaining admission to a college or university in the United States. However, as previously mentioned, to bring in the big bucks, you must be very intentional with the colleges to which you apply based on your SAT score. Regardless of your career goals and aspirations, I recommend that you align your SAT score with United States colleges and universities where you stand a good chance of getting the most scholarships and the cost to attend is not overly expensive.

By now, you should understand that we found ourselves among those SAT takers who did not see a significant increase in our SAT scores as needed to get a full scholarship, so we intentionally applied to colleges where there was at least a likelihood we could receive some type of scholarship. Obviously, the best place to be when it comes to college scholarships is receiving a full scholarship. Unfortunately, not every student will get a full scholarship, especially not every low-income student. If you cannot get a full scholarship, the next best is a college or university offering at least a 75-80% scholarship award. If that does not happen, then what is the next best thing? A college or university offering at least a 50% scholarship award. This is the least favorable position, but since it happens so often, it would be unrealistic for me not to include it in the discussion. If you cannot pay for college on your own and you are not able to secure a scholarship that covers all your college expenses, then you will reach a place where you begin to entertain the idea of applying for student loans. A student loan is the very last thing that you should think of. THE VERY LAST THING. Hence, this is the reason I have been stressing the importance of taking the time to diligently study for the SAT and apply to schools where your SAT score is competitive to bring in the scholarships you need.

Chapter VIII

Follow the Money

If you ask any of the Bramwell Triplets which United States college or university you should attend, we will undoubtedly tell you to pick the school that offers you the most in scholarships. In life, money is not all that matters. Still, when it comes down to deciding which United States college or university to attend, you should go to the school where you will pay the least out-of-pocket expenses, if any. The only time that this 'golden rule' will not apply is if you find yourself with equivalent scholarship offers from more than one school. Aside from that, youths, especially low-income youths, should seek schools that pay them to attend their school, and there are thousands of United States colleges and universities to choose from.

When the time comes for you to apply for college or university in the United States, it is essential that you are a top-tier student who can differentiate yourselves from other similarly situated students who share common life experiences with you. For example, many low-income students applying to college will come from homes and communities where they encounter difficult situations. This is almost guaranteed because life for many low-income students is filled with hardships and challenges. Many low-income students come from broken and financially unstable households where no one ever attended college. Some low-income students do not have a place to call home. Despite the economic woes and circumstances that low-income students encounter, these hardships are not enough to gain admission to a college or university in the United States, especially an admission letter with scholarships. You need organic stories demonstrating how you persevered and overcame your difficult situations.

Organic stories mean authentic stories—they must be your lived experiences. Given the value of organic stories to help differentiate you from other students, you must pay keen attention to how you spend your time inside and outside your high school classroom. You must be intentional with your time by actively engaging in extracurricular leadership activities early in high school.

When applying for college or university in the United States, you want to be in a position where your extracurricular leadership activities exemplify how you contributed to your high school community. By doing so, you can demonstrate that you are someone with the ability to make a meaningful contribution to your college community. Another important reason to make a meaningful contribution to your high school community is that it will help you when the time comes to ask your teachers/principal/guidance counselor to write you a letter of recommendation that you will submit as part of your United States college application. Most schools typically ask for two letters of recommendation, and you want to ensure the persons you choose know you personally and can write you a strong letter of recommendation that speaks highly of you as a learner and the value you brought to your high school community.

When I speak of colleges, I refer to undergraduate programs whereby students obtain their bachelor's degree in four years (or less if a student meets certain requirements to graduate early). There are different types of colleges. For example, Liberal Arts Colleges encourage students to develop an appreciation for many subjects (including humanities, arts, and social sciences) and practice their critical thinking skills. In addition to Liberal Arts Colleges, there are Historically Black Colleges and Universities (HBCUs). HBCUs are schools originally founded to provide higher education opportunities for Black Americans. Interestingly, when we applied to Saint Augustine's University, we did not know it was an HBCU. As HBCU alums, we can attest to the sense of camaraderie and diverse learning experience that HBCUs provide for international students.

When I speak of universities, I refer to four-year private or public organizations offering undergraduate and graduate programs. Generally, universities offer more research opportunities and are more prestigious than most colleges. Both the state governments and the federal government of the United States fund public universities. However, private universities mainly receive funding through tuition fees and endowments (i.e., large donations such as alumni donations). Schools with very large endowments are generally better positioned to fund international students freely. This is often limited to private colleges and universities. Public universities do not offer government-funded financial aid to international students. However, international students interested in attending a public university in the United States should investigate whether the respective public university offers tuition waivers for international students. A tuition waiver allows an international student to pay the in-state tuition (i.e., the rate American students pay to attend a public or state college or university in their state of residence) that local American students pay.

It is important to ensure the college and universities you apply to offer need-based and merit-based scholarships to international students. A merit-based scholarship is a type of financial aid based on a student's academic performance (including SAT score), leadership roles, and extracurricular activities. A need-based scholarship is exactly what it says. This scholarship is awarded to students who can demonstrate that they need financial aid to attend school. It is important to understand that most international students are not eligible to apply for need-based scholarships from the United States government, which is also known as the Free Application for Federal Student Aid (i.e., FAFSA). When I speak of international students, I refer to non-United States citizens or non-permanent residents (i.e., persons with a green card). There are, however, limited instances where non-United States citizens or non-permanent residents may be eligible to receive need-based financial assistance (for example, the 1789 Jay Treaty grants certain Native American students born in Canada the ability to receive government-funded financial aid). To learn more about the other instances where non-United States citizens can receive government-funded financial aid, I recommend you visit the Federal Student Aid website.

The eight most prestigious private universities in the United States are known as Ivy Leagues. The Ivy League comprises the following schools: Harvard University, Princeton University, Brown University, University of Pennsylvania, Columbia University, Dartmouth College, Yale University and Cornell University. It is important to keep in mind that Ivy League schools generally do not offer merit-based or athletic-based scholarships. With much slimmer acceptance rates than an average college or university in the United States, students admitted into Ivy League schools have already proven their academic and athletic merit. Although Ivy League schools do not offer full-ride merit-based scholarships, they still offer strong need-based financial aid programs.

When a United States college or a scholarship requires a prospective student to show 'demonstrated need' to receive need-based financial assistance, it refers to a student's total cost of attendance, less any amount that will be paid via contributions from others (including scholarship awards). The total cost of attendance refers to education expenses such as tuition fees and personal expenses (including student housing, books, and transportation) during a specific academic year). The cost of attendance can be demonstrated through school vouchers, rent receipts, personal expenses, and transportation expenses budget. Many United States colleges and universities require tuition money to balance their fiscal budgets and view international students as a major source of that funding. Therefore, this limits the amount of scholarship money they can furnish to international students.

For high school students who participate in extracurricular athletic activities (for example, track and field), note that there are United States colleges and universities that offer full-ride sports scholarships. Admittedly, these sports scholarships are fiercely competitive, and there are many rules about how students receive them. The good news is that international student-athletes have plenty of opportunities to pursue a college education in the United States by obtaining a sports scholarship. Some sports, for example, track and field, tennis, soccer, water polo, ice hockey, golf, and basketball, recruit international student-athletes more than others. Generally, international students who can obtain sports scholarships in the United States are not required to have competitive SAT scores as those seeking purely merit-based scholarships. In these circumstances, the United States colleges and universities offer prospective international student-athletes a full-ride sports scholarship, in exchange for having the students play on the school's respective sports teams. Therefore, decisive factor in providing such a scholarship is a student's abilities, not academic ones. Securing a full-ride schol international student-athlete usually entails cont directly, sending them statistics about your at' sharing videos of you playing a sport, and pa recruiting process. One of the keys to successi scholarship is to research your options and look for the right opportunities meticulously. Therefore, you should start your research at least a year before the date you plan to attend a college or university in the United States.

As a low-income Caribbean high school student interested in studying in the United States, it is extremely important to research and take advantage of the scholarship opportunities available to international students. For example, did you know that in 2012, Robyn Rihanna Fenty, a renowned Barbadian singer, created a scholarship program to help international students attend college in the United States? This scholarship program provided through the Clara Lionel Foundation is for international students who are citizens or natives of Barbados, Cuba, Haiti, Brazil, Grenada, Guyana, and Jamaica enrolled in an accredited four-year college or university in the United States. Applicants who are successful with the Clara Lionel Foundation scholarship program are awarded scholarships ranging from US$5,000.00 to $50,000.00. Once certain academic performance is maintained (for example, maintaining a certain grade point average each semester), the scholarship award may be renewed for three additional years or until the scholarship recipient receives his or her bachelor's degree. To learn more about Rhianna's scholarship program, I implore you to visit the Clara Lionel Foundation website and apply for the scholarship, if you are eligible.

Low-income Caribbean students who cannot obtain any merit-based, need-based, or sport-based scholarship but still desire to study in the United States must do what is in their best interest, given the stark realities of their situation. Studying in the United States is, by far, a great financial investment. Thus, even if you cannot obtain any scholarship, you should consider whether obtaining a loan to cover college expenses is in your best interest. Your degree from an accredited college or university in the United States undoubtedly opens global professional opportunities, which can result in high earning possibilities throughout your career. While the options may be fewer, student loans from private lenders (for example, MPower loans) can cover college or university expenses such as tuition fees, student housing, books, school, etc.

Should you go the route of obtaining a private loan, it is important that you ensure you understand the financial terms associated with the loan. Keep in mind that student loans can be crippling. Thus, it is important to only borrow what you need to cover your educational expenses.

Chapter IX

F-1 Student Do's and Don'ts

The United States college admissions process can be a rigorous and overwhelming journey for international students. Receiving a United States college admission letter, particularly one with a scholarship offer, makes the arduous journey worth it. As you pursue your studies in the United States, there are certain rules and regulations you should be aware of as an international student.

As an international student, you must obtain a non-immigrant F-1 student visa to enter the United States and commence your studies. The United States college or university you enroll in must be an accredited Student and Exchange Visitor Program (SEVP) certified institution. An accredited United States college or university means that an accrediting agency has recognized the school as an institution equipped with the resources necessary to provide a certain level of education. An accredited United States SEVP college or university is an institution that has received authorization from the United States government to accept/enroll international students. It is important to note that you cannot apply for the non-immigrant F-1 student visa until the accredited SEVP school sends you an acceptance/admission letter.

Once you are accepted to an accredited SEVP-certified university or college, you will receive an I-20 Form from your school official, referred to as the Designated School Official (DSO). The DSO is responsible for signing and delivering an I-20 Form to you. The I-20 Form proves that you are a legitimate student studying in the United States and is an important step in getting your F-1 student visa. There are two requirements that you must satisfy to obtain the I-20 Form. First, the college or university you applied to must accept your application, and the accredited institution must be SEVP-certified. Second, the college or university you are attending must confirm that your personal information (e.g., country of citizenship, name, and date of birth) is correct and that you have enough funds to cover your costs during your stay in the United States. Keep in mind that having enough funds to cover your stay in the United States is not limited to funds for your tuition but also includes cost of living expenses such as money for student housing. If you cannot prove that you have enough funds to cover your costs during your stay in the United States, your I-20 Form will not be issued.

Caribbean students with partial scholarships can offset their United States college or university expenses by attending schools in states where they have relatives who can provide housing sponsorship, and there is an easy mode of transportation. First-year college or university students at certain schools are allowed to dorm off-campus. For example, a colleague of mine resided with her godmother while at a college in Florida. By doing so, she did not have to show proof of funds for housing when she attended her student visa interview. Instead, she had to submit a letter of housing sponsorship.

Once your I-20 Form is approved, the DSO at your school will enter your information in the Student and Exchange Visitor Information System (SEVIS). To receive your F-1 student visa, you must pay an I-901 SEVIS fee, which is approximately US$350.00 (as of the publication date of this book). Although the I-20 Form will indicate the expected start date for your academic studies (i.e., your United

States college/university start date), the United States government permits F-1 students to enter the United States thirty days prior to that date.

When travelling to the United States, you must ensure you have your original I-20 Form with your signature to enter the country, and you will likely have to present it to a Customs and Border Protection officer upon arrival at the airport.

After receiving an I-20 Form from the school you plan to enroll in, you must complete a DS-160 visa application and pay the associated fees, which is approximately US$210.00 (as of the publication date of this book). During your F-1 student visa interview, you will likely need to bring the following: a valid certificate of eligibility—I-20 Form, proof of admission, a passport (valid at least six months into the future), evidence of financial support (including any scholarship award/sponsorship), visa application forms and fees, and SEVIS fee receipt. To obtain your F-1 student visa, you must show that you intend to return to your home country after completing your studies in the United States. This can be achieved by showing the interviewing immigration officer how you plan on using your degree upon return to your home country.

As an F-1 student in the United States, you must maintain your F-1 student visa by remaining compliant with applicable rule and regulations. Compliance can be achieved by maintaining the requirements and conditions as described in your F-1 student visa and your college or university codes of conduct and/or regulations. Essentially, you need to remember the purpose for which you entered the United States, which is to study.

One key regulation to be mindful of is the requirement to enroll in a full course of study each semester for the entirety of your study in the

United States. This is a very important rule that international students must be aware of because failure to maintain a full course of study could jeopardize your F-1 student status. While maintaining a full course load each semester, F-1 students are typically allowed to accept on-campus employment for up to 20 hours per week, and the work does not need to be related to your course of study. Suppose you are not going to a United States college or university on a full-ride scholarship (i.e., a scholarship that covers your entire college cost, such as tuition, housing, textbooks and meals), and your family lacks the financial resources to support you while studying (as was the case for us), in that case I strongly encourage you to consider attending a United States college or university that has on-campus employment available for F-1 students. When we applied to college in the United States, this was an area we overlooked. In the aggregate, our scholarships from Saint Augustine's University and GK/FGFS covered our tuition, housing, and meals (scholarships that cover on-campus meals generally enable you to receive breakfast, lunch, and dinner every day the school is open). However, our scholarships did not cover transportation, textbooks, clothes, or phone subscriptions. Therefore, working on campus was our only means to purchase what we needed to assist us in our studies.

My recommendation to seek out United States colleges and universities that offer on-campus employment may seem somewhat unorthodox. However, as a college student, particularly an F-1 student, you will undoubtedly need money for seen and unforeseen expenses, regardless of the scholarship you receive. Some college students resort to taking out loans to cover their living expenses. As I have mentioned in previous chapters, you may consider taking on debt only after you have exhausted all other options. However, the ability to work on-campus will still be beneficial as it reduces the amount you may need to borrow, no matter how modest the compensation might be.

Throughout the preceding chapters, I have reiterated that the higher your SAT score is, the more competitive your United States college application is, which will position you to get more scholarship money. The more scholarship money, the merrier, right? Undoubtedly, yes, and in case you have forgotten, the goal is always to secure the most scholarships.

Truthfully, no matter how inspired and informed you might be by reading this book—which I hope you are—it will not guarantee that you will ace the SAT and get a full-ride scholarship to a college or university in the United States. From a practical viewpoint, while some international students can secure a full academic or student-athlete scholarship, some international students will receive only partial or no scholarships. You must find a middle ground when goals and reality are not aligned. The middle ground between goals and reality is practicality. International students who only receive partial scholarships to study in the United States need pragmatic solutions to cover their outstanding college balance. One way of financially supporting oneself in college is working while studying. Attending United States colleges and universities that offer on-campus employment to international students with partial scholarships is a strategic choice to help lessen one's financial burden. Additionally, colleges and universities that offer work aid are likely invested in international student affairs.

We were extremely fortunate to obtain on-campus employment throughout our university tenure. However, we attended a relatively small HBCU that generally did not offer on-campus employment to F-1 students. Therefore, the fact that we could work on campus at our HBCU was the exception and not the norm. If you can, I implore you to seek out a United States college or university where on-campus employment for F-1 students is the norm and not the exception. Admittedly, this will likely not be practical for students with certain scholarships. For example, student-athlete scholarships generally do not allow on-campus employment while studying. Due to student-athlete's schedules, this prohibition seems reasonable. Similarly, students with full-ride academic scholarships to college or university in the United States generally are not allowed to work on campus. For students who are United States citizens or permanent residents, this may not be a major issue because these students still have the option to work off-campus. Unfortunately, F-1 students do not have this privilege. For F-1 students with full-ride scholarships or families with the financial resources to support them with any related miscellaneous expenses while studying (e.g., rent for housing during holidays), not being able to work is less concerning.

It is imperative that F-1 students with full-ride scholarships to college or university in the United States maintain a panoramic perspective on college, notwithstanding the lack of financial support from their immediate family. With a full-ride academic scholarship, you are likely not eligible to work on-campus, and you also cannot work off-campus due to your F-1 student visa restrictions. These restrictions severely limit your ability to earn money on campus to cover any miscellaneous expenses. However, I encourage you to think creatively and consider the talents or skills you could market while studying on campus. For example, Colleen was a very good hairstylist, and she was able to earn additional money as a hairstylist serving fellow students. Similarly, there was a talented make-up artist student at our HBCU, and she earned money from doing other students' makeup. If there is a specific subject that you are good at, you could consider offering tutoring sessions to students at a cost. I want you to make the best of your situation while complying with your school's code of conduct and your F-1 student visa rules.

The F-1 student visa permits off-campus employment in limited circumstances when a student can prove that he or she needs to work off-campus while studying due to unforeseen hardship. With a full-ride scholarship, meeting this unforeseen hardship criteria will be difficult due to the presumption that your full-ride scholarship covers all your college expenses. However, this is not an impossible task.

In addition to part-time on-campus employment, the United States government allows F-1 students to engage in Curricular Practical Training (CPT) which is required to complete an academic course of study. Academic courses requiring practical training (i.e., CPT) are generally found in practical courses where students gain more by applying their studies in the workplace, such as business and engineering courses. CPT essentially authorizes F-1 students to gain employment training. Therefore, when you think of CPT, think of paid internships that can be full-time or part-time and off-campus or on-campus. Keep in mind that to qualify as CPT, your academic course of study must require employment. If work training is optional in your academic course of study, you will not be eligible for CPT. Additionally, CPT only applies to major programs of study. Therefore, if you have a minor that requires work training, you will not be allowed to use CPT to meet this requirement.

Alternatively, international students can participate in Optional Practical Training (OPT), which is a 1-year employment authorization at each degree level (e.g., bachelor's degree and master's degree). There are two kinds of OPT: pre-completion and post-completion. This employment authorization can be used either before completion of studies during annual vacation or leave term (i.e., pre-completion OPT) or after completion of studies (i.e., post-completion OPT). Completion of studies is defined as the actual date you complete all requirements for a program of study (such as the date of your final exams). It is not automatically considered to be the date of graduation ceremonies. You do not need to secure an offer of employment before applying for OPT, and you can work anywhere in the United States. You may also change employment during your OPT period. However, similar to CPT, both pre-completion and post-completion OPT must be related to your bachelor's degree or field of study.

When applying for pre-completion OPT, F-1 students must consider certain timing guidelines. First, F-1 students must enroll full-time for one academic year at a college or university prior to applying for pre-completion OPT. Second, F-1 students can submit their application for pre-completion OPT to the United States Citizens and Immigration Services (USCIS) up to ninety days before fulfilling the one-year academic requirement. The authorization process takes an average of 3-5 months; therefore, you should submit your application as early as possible. However, before applying to USCIS, you must request an OPT recommendation from your DSO (designated school official). This is an official notice to USCIS that you satisfy the requirements to receive off-campus employment. Once approved, you will receive an updated I-20 Form from your DSO with a recommendation for you to participate in OPT. Ensure that you sign the updated I-20 Form before submitting it to USCIS. You must submit your pre-completion OPT request to USCIS within thirty days of the date that your updated I-20 Form is issued.

When applying for post-completion OPT, F-1 students can submit their post-completion OPT application ninety days prior to the academic program completion date stipulated on their I-20 Form or within sixty days after the academic program completion date on the I-20 Form. If you fail to apply for post-completion OPT within this window, you essentially forfeit your opportunity to benefit from employment after completion of your studies in the United States. Regardless of the OPT that you apply for (i.e., pre-completion or post-completion), it is unlawful to begin working before you receive your OPT employment authorization card (EAD) and the effective start date listed on the EAD has been reached. Furthermore, you cannot continue working beyond the effective end date listed on the EAD unless you have received a valid work authorization extension. F-1 students with a degree in Science, Technology, Engineering or Mathematics (STEM) can apply for an OPT extension from USCIS that permits them to work an additional twenty-four months in occupations related to their STEM degree.

Pre-completion and post-completion OPT provides an incredible opportunity for F-1 students to gain valuable work experience in the United States. Therefore, I wholeheartedly recommend you take full advantage of OPT while maintaining your F-1 student visa status. Since OPT generally authorizes employment for only twelve months for each degree level, you need to be strategic when using your OPT. If you choose to use pre-completion OPT during your annual summer breaks before completing your studies, it will reduce the time you can work full-time after your studies. For example, let's imagine that at the end of your second year in college, you receive an 8-week summer employment related to your field of study and decide to accept the employment. This is an amazing opportunity because you are gaining work experience and earning money. The disadvantage to this scenario is that it will reduce your post-completion OPT time to approximately ten months, since you have already used eight weeks out of the allotted twelve months of OPT time. An advantage to working on OPT is that you may receive a tax refund, if applicable, which you can use to further assist you with any financial needs that may arise while studying.

Generally, if you earn money in the United States, you pay a certain percentage in taxes. You pay taxes to the federal and state governments where you reside. For tax purposes, F-1 students are mainly classified as nonresident aliens and are required to file a tax return (form 1040-NR) for income earned from sources in the United States (such as wages and salaries). Therefore, F-1 students with employment or paid internships through OPT or CPT will be required to pay United States taxes. Tax returns detailing your income are usually due in April each year. Once you start working, you will likely be required to complete the IRS Form W-4 Employee's Withholding Certificate, which allows your employer to assess your liabilities for taxes. In return, your employer will provide you with the IRS Form W-2 Wages and Tax Statement indicating the earnings you received and the withheld taxes. If the Internal Revenue Service (IRS) determines that you paid an excess amount in taxes to the government, you will receive a tax refund. If you have paid less money in taxes than you owe, you are responsible for paying the difference. Even if you did not earn any income while studying, you will likely have to at least file the IRS Form 8843, Statement for Exempt Individuals and Individuals with Medical Condition, for each calendar year that you are in the United States to remain compliant with your F-1 student visa obligations.

Working in the United States after graduating from college or university is an option for F-1 students, and as mentioned previously, F-1 students can work on OPT for each level of their degree. Graduating from undergraduate (i.e., college or university) is considered a separate degree level from completing graduate school (for example, completing law school and obtaining your juris doctorate). As I discussed previously, OPT only authorizes employment for 1-year (unless you can get the STEM extension mentioned previously). For F-1 students in the United States desiring to obtain employment in the United States beyond the typical 1-year OPT period, a work visa sponsored by an employer can be a great resource for employment in the country. An example of a work visa sponsored by an employer is the H-1B visa. The H-1B visa is a nonimmigrant visa generally granted for three years but, under certain circumstances, can be extended for an additional three years. H-1B visa allows F-1 students to receive work related to their specialty occupation. A specialty occupation is essentially an occupation requiring a bachelor's degree (or its equivalent). Examples of specialty occupations include education, accounting, law, architecture, engineering, mathematics, medicine, and health.

H-1B visa sponsorship allows you to change your legal status from international student to foreign professional. Unlike OPT, which allows F-1 students to apply for work authorization on their own, F-1 students must find an employer that will petition for the H-1B visa from the United States government on their behalf. Typically, 65,000 H-1B visas are issued annually for non-United States citizens or permanent residents holding a bachelor's degree (or equivalent), while 20,000 H-1B visas are issued for those with higher degrees (i.e., a master's degree or doctoral). With the limited H-1B visas available, it is important that your employer files for the H-1B visas as soon as possible.

In addition to H-1B visas, there are other options for F-1 students to obtain employment in the United States after graduating college or university by securing an EB-2 or EB-3 employment visa. The requirements to obtain an EB-2 or EB-3 employment visa differ from the H1-B visa requirements. If you wish to work in the United States beyond the allotted OPT period, you need to research the requirements of each visa to determine which option is best for you.

Now that I have shared how my sisters and I achieved our dream and became two lawyers and one doctor, it is your turn to shine like the star you are. Go and make your dream a reality; if we did it, so can you.

Supplemental Materials

As a supplement to your purchase of the book *Two Lawyers One Doctor: Breaking Barriers to Achieve Success*, you can receive a free copy of the Calculated Chance Checklist, a reference guide on the essential steps you should take to study in the United States on scholarships.

To request your free copy of the Calculated Chance Checklist, please send an email to Bramwelltriplets@gmail.com.

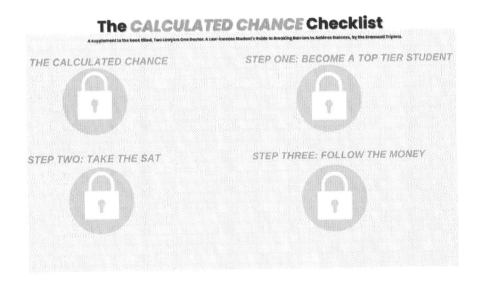

Please note: This will be provided as a free supplement to the book only upon request.

About the Author

Cadine Bramwell is the firstborn of the Bramwell Triplets from Tivoli Gardens, West Kingston, Jamaica. After graduating from Tivoli Gardens high school, Cadine and her sisters (Colleen and Colliet) attended Saint Augustine's University in Raleigh, North Carolina, on scholarships and graduated with high honors. Cadine then attended the Maurica A. Deane School of Law at Hofstra University in Hempstead, New York. Cadine is currently a practicing attorney in the United States.

Made in the USA
Middletown, DE
17 February 2024

49943026R00071